WALKERGEMS

GET YOUR A$% OFF THE COUCH

By April Walker

Thank you
for taking time
to read my book
of these

Jesus loving you
Continued Blessings

April Walker

ISBN: 1542484782
ISBN-13: 9781542484787

CONTENTS

To Montana, Greg, Sophie, and Skye

"What you think, you will become.

Think you're great because you are."

In memory of Reggie Osse'

We live in the most amazing time. You can literally create a biz, living anywhere in the world, and work from your laptop or phone with a dollar and a dream. It all starts with believing that you can.

INTRODUCTION

We all have different DNA and are wired intricately... understood. We won't all be entrepreneurs. Some of us may want to be a part of the process and decide to be a team player instead of the CEO, while others will live on the edge and were born to take risks every day. Either way, whichever one you are, if you don't plan your life, your life will designate a plan for you, but it just might not be the one you want.

I remember being on my journey at 20 with no blueprint and no mentor. There was no one there at the beginning of my climb. I needed that. We all do. I hope that this book can help you on that climb and that it serves as the hand to help push you up your mountain. God plants seeds in us and wants us to grow them. Our biggest gifts are often the ones that are most overlooked. It took me almost a decade to get comfortable with the fact that I really was a fashion designer. I don't think I was comfortable with that title because of my insecurities. There were voices inside that told me, "You don't have formal training, you're fooling yourself," or "Why me?" At the same time, this fashion thing was the very thing that was keeping me up at night, making me wake up early in the morning, work 16-hour days...not even realizing how much time flew by. It was that one thing that I WANTED to do.

I didn't mind for many years that the grind didn't add up to the numbers in my bank account because there was a driving force....my passion, my purpose, my focus, and my ability to see the unseen and believe the unbelievable. In hindsight, that was God shining a little light down the tunnel, keeping me on track to stay the course. Don't get it twisted, in the midst of this journey were big bursts of trials, mixed with struggle, doubt, crisis, breakthroughs, growth, and success. It was all part of a divine plan.

Leveling up means at every stage of your growth, you will be challenged. Don't go through it, but grow through it. With every epiphany and vision, you will be stretched and taken out of your comfort zone. Think of it as prep school. It gives us our foundation, provides the life lessons, and hopefully keeps our feet on solid ground. I remember when I opened my first shop, called Fashion in Effect. The first year open, I broke my leg, and I wasn't able to be there for a few months. We were still trying to get off the ground, and there were months where the outflow was still greater than the inflow. I can recall there was one month the electric bill was due and we didn't have the money to pay it and my teammate, Randy, didn't want to stress me out further by telling me (so the lights went out). God bless him. That same day a good customer happened to stop by our shop and left the money to turn the lights on and told my teammate not to tell me. Sometimes when you don't know how it will happen, but trust the process, and the answers and solutions will appear.

I've learned to be humble. It gives you a better perspective in life, especially if you're an entrepreneur. When you understand that you may fail more times than you win and you're OK with that possibility, then you're on the right track. When you can look at failure as a growth lesson or use those perceived failures as stepping-stones to move forward toward success, it's not failure. Failure is only when the book is finished and you've finished with your last chapter. You still have chapters left to create. Your faith needs to be stronger than your fear. My willingness to be a long-distance runner, and keep going despite getting knocked down, makes my success story. It's made me stronger and wiser and gives me foresight for the road ahead.

If I can do it, YOU CAN, too. Whatever you really want, you can manifest as long as you believe it, and move those mountains out of your head. You are the only person who can write your own ticket by believing in yourself, paying attention, tapping into your gift, nurturing it, and the most important part... getting started. Hone your skills, but remember, if you wait for perfection you will never start. I started thirty years ago and am still constantly learning, shaping, growing, reinventing.

It's definitely an evolutionary process. Whether you're working for someone else and want to be a better team player, whether you're the captain of your own ship... if you're sixteen or sixty, these #walkergems are created for you to increase your faith, as one big love note, to awaken your potential, with sprinklings of information and inspiration for the journey.

Let me be clear, I'm sharing from my perspective, and through the lens of my experience. This is not a "my way or the highway" book. Take what you can from it and feel free to retool accordingly in order to fit your blueprint. Also, this book can serve as an excellent "refresher" book, for those who have already become successful at what they do, or simply to serve as a reminder or to get that second wind.

#BYOB

WHAT DO YOU WANT TO BE WHEN YOU GROW UP?

I often wonder, if people could be anything in the world, what would they want to be? I decided to do a Facebook survey, and many people had different answers from their existing jobs or situations. Here are some of the answers below.

Pamela Morton	Archaeologist
Yolanda Wilson	Elementary gym teacher
Akkitta W. Copelin	Celebrity stylist
Roget Romain	Professor
Darwin Sealey	Shaman/griot/healer
Ernest Eans Jr.	Working w/ NY Jets/Giants
Kari Cunningham	Event planning & present job
Melli Mel	Marketing and promotion
Fahja Bey	Marriage and family therapist
Tony Vestal	Clothing/brand ambassador
Giovanni Ocasio	Music producer/philanthropy
Carabronze	Fashion designer/psychiatrist
Robert Poppel	Run a women's shelter
Buddha Bless	Comedian, author
Mark Montgomery	Work with the NBA
Mark N. Hardy	Legendary oil painter

WALKERGEMS

LaTanya Kellogg   Author, singer, and designer

Sherri Guishard   Pilot

Ross Guilty   Songwriter

What would you decide to be?

Did you know that I was in the pet business? The year after 9/11, I opened an all-natural pet boutique called the Walker Pet Shop, located in Brooklyn and offering unique services, products, and accessories. I was convinced I was going to catch the wave of new pet owners with disposable incomes in the evolving metamorphosis of gentrification occurring in my hood. I know in hindsight, opening right after 9/11 was a terrible time to open a new business. Give me a second chance and I would make a different decision, considering all of those variables, but at that time, I just knew it would be a win-win. Sometimes you have to take the risk, but always do feasibility studies and assess the risk and variables. No one knew what long-term effects 9/11 would have on business in our country. Ultimately, because of several factors, I closed my pet shop four years later. I could consider it a failure, but it served as a great test market for the pet business. I received the lesson. It definitely was a costly one, but it was a chapter in my book and a part of my journey. You're not going to win them all, but you have to keep swinging.

April Walker

WE ALL HAVE SEEDS INSIDE OF US, WITH SOMETHING UNIQUE AND SPECIAL TO THE WORLD.

We are born to plant, cultivate, and grow these seeds, while watching the maturation process. This process determines how we "pay and play" in this life. As Les Brown stated, "Too many of us aren't living our dreams because we are living our fears." You need to plot, plow, and build. You may have a passion as an artist but be sitting in an office, or maybe you're an artist, but it's a deferred dream. You may have dreams of traveling the world and taking pictures in each place and blogging about it, or have a love for fashion with tons of style, but you haven't embraced it as a skill, or maybe you just want to help others build businesses and win or become a brand evangelist. Whatever you imagine, we have never lived in a better time than now to pursue our dreams. With the tools and technology of today, it can be real.

The playing field is wide open if you swing with aim. "The Anatomy of an Entrepreneur," a report produced in 2009 by the Ewing Marion Kauffman Foundation for entrepreneurship gathered some interesting facts that I'd like to share and may inspire you.

1. The average and median age of company founders when they started their first business was 40.

2. The majority of the entrepreneurs in the sample were serial entrepreneurs. The average number of businesses launched by respondents was approximately 2.3.

3. The majority of respondents (75.4 percent) had worked as employees at other companies for more than six years before launching their own companies.

4. Entrepreneurship doesn't always run in the family. More than half (51.9 percent) of respondents were the first in their families to launch a business.

5. 69.9% were married when they started their first business.

There are pros and cons for everyone in starting a business. Young people have a lot of great ideas and energy and can assume a lot more risks because their lives are usually very different at 20 versus 40. They also see the world differently. At the same time, silver foxes and seasoned human beings have their own advantages. They have an edge…it's called experience. Experience gives people more humility and leadership, management, and team-building skills, so whatever age you are, you can start where you are.

So many of us "exist instead of insist." Insist on your dream if you have one, insist on giving it your all.

Once you know your DNA, move forward with a sense of urgency. Map a plan. For example, if you have a job, maybe that job will be what ends up acting as an investor to fund your dream. Be proactive and plan carefully and be. Dreams don't become real without our own participation.

The THINKS You Can Think!

—Dr. Seuss

HAPPINESS IS A STATE OF MIND AND A CHOICE.

It's also an inward and outward process. There are three categories…your mentality, spirituality, and physicality. When properly aligned, these three work in tandem to create a beautiful human experience.

Everyone should be crystal clear about these four things:

o What do you love to do?

o Are you clear about your value system?

o What kind of life do you want to create?

o What kind of legacy do you want to leave with this world?

A lot of us don't get to think about this or take the time to know ourselves because we're too busy living to please other people and living up to someone else's expectations. We're in survival mode, and as a result we're in a reactionary state. We never take the time to get to know ourselves, but when we spend time with ourselves, it's amazing what we can discover.

Here are some suggestions.

Write down what comes easy to you…what is effortless?

Now close your eyes. Envision your dream life.

In a perfect world, describe a perfect day. What would that look like?

What does it feel like?

Where would you live?

Are you single? Married? Do you want a family?

BYOB, career or enterprise?

How do you want to serve others?

These questions will help you gain some clarity and paint your picture.

Your mind will answer most questions if you learn to relax and wait for the answers.

- William S. Burroughs

Staying positive in this world takes effort. It means constant checks and balances and possibly changing the trajectory of our thoughts. Just like weeds grow in the garden, they seep into our lives, and it's up to us to be conscious of them and extract them. Weeds can pull us down, dull our senses, hinder potential growth, and kill the vision. Stay on top of your gardens by watering and feeding them with the right tools to keep them vibrant.

IT'S NEVER TOO LATE.

IF YOU DON'T LIKE

YOUR REALITY, CHANGE

IT

AGE AIN'T NOTHING BUT A NUMBER.

-Aaliyah

Mark Zuckerberg started Facebook at 19

Colonel Sanders started Kentucky Fried Chicken at 72

Evan Spiegel started Snapchat at 22

Nathan Blecharczyk- cokickstarted Airbnb at 24

Lynn Brooks started Big Apple Greeter at 59

Daymond John started FUBU at 23 years old.

Sidney Frank started Grey Goose Vodka at 77

Whether you're young or seasoned, there are no excuses.

READY?

DISRESPECT YOUR CURRENT STATUS

You have to be willing to disrespect your current status. You need to shake things up, upset your routine, and put a shock into your system. Changing your current address means being prepared to occupy a new space. Your present mental space doesn't have enough capacity for the thoughts or behavior that are needed for your future address. In other words, be damn disrespectful to your present address. Get ready to move.

Quick reference story - There is no better teacher than experience. When I launched my first business, it was on a shoestring budget, with a homemade awning sign that we made ourselves. We made a lot of mistakes in the beginning, but we learned, gained experience, and as a result, increased our confidence, leveling up. When I first started Walker Wear, I had to step out on faith. I was 21.

I packed my bags and headed to explore L.A. to find domestic production. I stayed at my father's friend's house for three months until I could get my own place. The house was close to Rollin 60s Crips turf in L.A, Hyde Park, and this was back in 1989. On top of that I was an East Coaster, so I felt like a fish out of water.

It was such a different landscape. I didn't know anyone in L.A. and I didn't have any real experience yet in fashion, but I would still get in my rent-a-car every day and go to the fashion district, networking, poking around, finding out about factories, visiting them, and acting like I belonged there. In order to make moves, I had to abandon my norm and current "mental address" and be willing to move in an unfamiliar zone and with a new landscape. We can't keep doing the same thing with the same people, in the same safe places, and expect different results.

Start with what you have. Manage this first stage well. The beginning is the foundational phase that you can never skip, and it also serves as great test marketing. Invest in your dream in growth stages. Taking it in stages allows you to master every part well before you take it up a notch. Leveling up and adding layers allow you to absorb and scale, and gives you a better "recovery rate." I'm glad I wasn't able to start at the top because I was really green. I had little knowledge and no experience; therefore, I never could've sustained my fashion business. I would've made huge and costly mistakes that risked it all, because I didn't take the time to "go and grow" through the process. The process is there for a reason. There's a reason and a season. Think of it as your sailboat to your destination. It's also where you'll discover how to sustain your dream.

I try to constantly occupy "new residencies," challenge myself by leveling up and setting new benchmarks. I challenge you to ask yourself, what can you do to occupy a new residency and take yourself out of the comfort zone? Take a class, begin lessons, join a Toastmasters club, or try something new to mix it up, discover something new, whether it's a photography or writing class, going back to school, or becoming an activist! Consider waking up an hour earlier and going to bed an hour later to dedicate time to your dream, especially if you're a day-gigger. This will keep you passionate and feeling alive, and by adding this new thought process, your vision will keep magnifying over time. If you want more, you have to become more. Remember, it's never too late to change your course.

#goandgrow2gether

THAT THING THAT YOU ARE RUNNING AWAY FROM IS THE THING THAT MAKES YOU SPECIAL.

We all have a special magic inside of us, but our gifts don't always come in shiny packages with pretty bow ties. There's a thing inside of you that makes you special, but it's often overlooked because it comes to you with such ease. Maybe you're really lucky and have a few different talents. Life is pretty simple, but we make it complex. We over think it, kill the creativity and block the natural flow. It usually takes us a minute to recognize or own our gifts. Our biggest assets are within us, but many of us go through life chasing our tails because we think it can't be that obvious. We doubt our potential and end up selling ourselves short. When we're not in alignment with our gifts and don't have clarity, it's easy for doubt to seep into our lives. We become insecure because we're not sure.

We all have something to share with the world. It's a special quality inside of you that no one can take away from you but you. In a strange way, if you don't use it, you can lose it. Just as we exercise or use our brains to elevate our consciousness and minds, we have to use our gifts to make them sharper, brighter, and stronger, otherwise they dull and weaken, and we lose confidence. A lot of us start out in life with big dreams and have a sense of our gifts, but then after we get kicked down a few times, we forget or give up and end up settling for mediocrity. It's never too late for a change.

If you're tapping into your gifts, that's great. If you're not, have the COURAGE to move forward in faith and expectancy. Identify your gifts and claim them. Go for it. Remember who you are. That thing inside of you that makes you special is your greatest asset. Once you tap into your gifts, the universe will conspire to assist you. Greatness is something that shapes itself over time.

Speak it. Claim it. Own it. It's yours.

***When I first started #walkergems, it was intended as a freemium video to give extra value to my fashion brand. I wanted to give my online community something extra, by sharing my experience. This idea became my obsessive passion and working on it became the most exciting part of my day. I found myself spending more and more time working on its content and had a strong desire to connect, amplify, and ignite the spirit of entrepreneurship for as many people as possible. That one little freemium snowballed into a much bigger vision. The confirmation that I received from my audience let me know I'm on the right path. If I wasn't paying attention, I could have really missed an opportunity to serve and connect. We have to be courageous enough to share our gifts with the world.

April Walker

"It is not another person's responsibility to believe in your dreams. It's yours."

April Walker

SOMEDAY IS A WORD THAT KILLS DREAMS EVERY DAY.

Fear seeps into our lives somewhere, we become paralyzed. We wait for approval to step forward. Being stagnant is a form of risk taking as well. If you're not taking any action and hoping for a different result, you'll be disappointed. Have you ever been so busy being busy but still not getting ahead? When is the last time that you stopped to think about what you can do to change your circumstances? If we're honest, some of us are afraid to try because we're afraid to succeed. Succeeding would make us accountable and requires change and sustainability. We can always find justifiable obstacles or excuses to prevent us from moving forward. You can push past them and knock them down. The biggest challenge you'll have is to get out of your own way. The biggest barriers in life are psychological. Change starts with faith. Faith starts with belief. Beliefs ignite action. Our actions can move us forward in life or hold us back. Remember the lion in The Wizard of Oz? The lion lacked faith and didn't believe that he had the heart or courage, so he was looking everywhere else. He didn't know he had it the whole time! A lot of us are like that. Your dreams should scare you or they're not big enough. We must find courage to blaze a new path by equipping ourselves with passion, purpose, information, and the tools we need to experience our best lives imaginable. Let's get started.

FEAR IS A LIAR

ADDRESS THE ELEPHANT IN THE ROOM BY DEFLATING IT.

Demystify the bogeyman by turning on the lights. When you deal with the things that intimidate you, you take away the power.

When you have fear in any area, the first thing is to understand is why because you can identify it and then create solutions. Take the bull by the horns. Pick a fear association and keep pushing yourself to face and deal with it repetitively until it becomes less intimidating and you dispel the myth. This is how I've conquered fear in my life, by making it small. When we take action, it liberates us, building confidence, and in the process, we're empowered because we grow. Take your power back by turning on those lights. I have some success stories but more failures to share. They've made me stronger, wiser, they've opened new doors, and best of all, they've given me gems to pass on through my experience. Fear has a way of killing so many dreams, way more than failure ever will, because failure takes some form of action. We can learn lessons from failure, but fear keeps many from ever starting. Fear can come from unwanted past memories that block future opportunities, or sometimes it's just fear of the unknown. The reality is that most of what you fear will never take place. These are obstructive thoughts that hold us back.

According to the Small Business Administration, about two-thirds of businesses with employees survive at least two years and about half survive at least five years. Surprisingly, it's largely the internal factors and not external reasons that cause many businesses to fail. I believe that" fear can be the greatest obstructionist for success and the greatest enabler for failure."

Success is most often achieved by those who don't know that failure is inevitable.

—Coco Chanel

FAITH

OVER

FEAR

LET YOUR FAITH BE BIGGER THAN YOUR FEARS.

Faith is tested. God never closes one door without opening a new one. Discomfort and doubt may be a sign that a change is approaching. He'll take us out of our comfort zone to prepare us for a new season. When storms arrive, it gets dark, and everything gets flooded and is blown out of its place. In the midst of the storm, stillness, open ears, and a thankful heart will get you "to and through" with clarity for the road ahead. Eventually the sun always peeks out, bringing bright light, new horizons, and sometimes even a rainbow in the sky. Realize that your pain could be your remedy. When we hit a pain point, that's when our faith is tested. There is a lesson and a blessing in the pain. Introspective intelligence, looking in the mirror, doing the work, will help us find the answers. Being sensitive enough to snatch the lesson is paramount to growth. As change is often prompted by a crisis, it usually reveals something that we need to learn, address, change or work out, and through that experience, we become the seasoned veterans. From the caterpillar to the butterfly…don't go through it, but grow through it. Replacing fear with faith empowers us through the process. It also reminds us "this too shall pass." It's par for the course in preparing for a new season.

VISUALIZE A NEW CHAPTER.

A visualization exercise

Instead of thinking what if it doesn't work, I close my eyes most mornings and allocate at least seven minutes of time to visualize, with some visualization music playing, what I am manifesting and want to bring to life.

When you want to manifest and stay positive, there is power in painting the picture with clarity. Bring it to life, envisioning and setting the intention of that day, your actions and desired results. Some days I celebrate what the win feels like, how it feels at the debut of my film series, or how I feel when people tell me they have my book and really enjoyed reading it, or whatever I'm visualizing, I make it crystal clear with specificity. I allow myself a safe, quiet, and peaceful space to visualize. When I visualize, I'm present to what it feels like, from waking up throughout the actions of that whole day, attaching my feelings of triumph, joy, gratitude, and peace. In my mind, I'm constantly reaffirming my actions and letting these thoughts sink into my bones. I'm increasing faith and expectancy and manifesting. Eventually it becomes easier to believe, accept, and walk the walk. The dream becomes the reality. It's just a matter of time.

I've shared a link to the visualization music / exercise, but there are so many that exist to choose from. Repetition brings clarity.

God did not teach you how to swim just to let you drown.

—Andy Andrews

NOTE - Below is a link to the visualization exercise that I practice daily but there are tons of good ones to check out. Try different ones until you find what works for you.

My Morning Visualization Exercise

https://www.youtube.com/watch?v=856BTxtPW80

Every week, I also go to @urbanasanas for my yoga sessions in Brooklyn. If you're in Brooklyn, Jyll is the best.

RESISTING. Eagles never put their nest close to the ground—they're always positioned at high heights. Since the eaglets never want to leave the nest and refuse to learn how to fly, the eagle will force them with a surprise by breaking the nest and throwing the eaglet in the air. As cruel as it seems, the eagle is always close by. The eagle watches the eaglets as they try to flap their wings and then they'll swoop down and save them before they hit the ground. God treats us the same way. If we "resist our shift," he'll throw us up in the air to teach us how to fly, but he will always catch our fall. Have faith to learn how to fly in your new season.

#newseason #faith #mercy

SHIFTING. Once you acknowledge that you're ready, you need to shift. It's part of the development process. Most of us try to resist a shift. God will stick a fork in our side, nudge our discomfort, and keep working on us until we do. We can't change staying in the same place. It's like when you're flying on economy and you get your name on the standby list. Whenever your name is called, you need to move in order to get your seat. You have to be ready for the shift. Understanding the shifting process prepares us for new seasons. The seasons are designed to stretch us. They help us evolve and grow us into new areas of life. Know that trials don't come without blessings attached. In the meantime, there's an alignment that needs to happen of our physical, mental, and spiritual components in order to get us moving in the right way.

On that note, I want to leave you with James 1:2-4: "Consider it pure joy, my brothers and sisters, whenever you face trials of many kinds, because you know that the testing of your faith produces perseverance."

Winning and defeating both start in the mind.

THERE IS NO ONE WHO CAN QUANTIFY YOUR POTENTIAL AND THERE IS NO ONE WHO CAN MEASURE YOUR MIRACLES...NO ONE BUT YOU AND GOD.

I once attended a service at Emmanuel Baptist Church and heard a great sermon that spoke to me. There will always be pundits, analysts, and naysayers, but you have the ability to make them yaysayers. It all starts in your mind. Being mediocre is a lot more common than being mighty. There are many "good" and "mediocre" folks in the world—few stand out because it's easier to blend in. You were born to shine. Aspiration for greatness is the road less traveled, because it requires more work and is more challenging. A lot of times we talk ourselves out of greatness, because complacency and mediocrity seem to be easier routes. It's easier...I mean, it takes a certain amount of courage to be different, to dare to follow those dreams and defy the odds. It all comes down to our belief in our potential.

Now faith is the substance of things hoped for, the evidence of things not seen.

-Hebrews 11:1

Retrain your thoughts. You need to constantly feed your mind with positive, loving affirmations because you're listening. The way you think and feel about yourself will be crucial to your experience. Guard your heart and thoughts. It's hard to breed positive results when you're still thinking and feeling negative things. You have to work to keep positive with an open heart (from the moment you wake up to the time you go to sleep), which is challenging in today's world.

Here are a few tricks I use.

A) Give thanks. When I open my eyes, I give thanks that I woke up.

B) Devotional time

C) Gratitude

D) Remind yourself of three qualities that you love about yourself.

E) Honor yourself by investing in your health. Exercise regularly.

F) Make positive affirmations.

G) Filtration system: Be conscious of what you're taking in on a daily basis, from the music you listen to the media that is your entertainment to your relationships.

Stay surrounded by positive people that give good energy. Choose to be around people who will encourage you and are uplifting.

#circleup

as long as you're still mourning the past, you can't celebrate the future

-April Walker

WALKER

GETTING STARTED NOW IS INFINITELY MORE IMPORTANT THAN HOW YOU START.

Self-development should be a constant force in your life. The more we know, the more we grow. The more you learn, the more you can earn. Take yourself out of your safe box. Level up. Add something to mix it up—maybe it's something you want to learn or a new place you want to visit. Find ways to keep sprouting, by adding a new discovery, being open to a new thought process, developing a new trade or skill that can enhance your life, whether it's personally or professionally. Be the captain of your ship. Too many of us are drifting. Someday is the enemy of many dreams. Tomorrow isn't promised, so make sure to share your gift, talent, and passion with the world while you have a chance. Don't worry about getting it all right in the beginning because no one does. There is no "perfect plan," but at that moment you decide to lean into it, the world will conspire to assist you.

It's hard to tell the difference between a second chance or the last chance, so in this life you have to give it 100 percent and go for it. When you do this, you're living in your truth and you won't have regrets. You'll never have to second-guess yourself or think "maybe if I would've or could've," because you gave it your all. That's all anyone can do. When you do your best, a few things happen, you build your character, and you sleep better at night. The right opportunity will eventually manifest itself when you're open and ready to receive it.

Don't disrespect the development process. Never be an amateur about your life or capabilities. Being lazy is not sexy.

People will judge you, and competition is thick out here. You need to reach your full potential every time to design the best blueprint of your life. You get what you give and you only have this life to live.

Remember to keep giving yourself new benchmarks. If you're comfortable, then maybe it's time to shake it up.

I am the greatest; I said that even before I knew that I was.

-Muhammad Ali

YOUR WORDS WILL CREATE YOUR WORLD.

Our words have power, and they can speak life or death, victory or defeat, and success or failure. If we master our minds, we dictate our words that give life to our world.

Your thoughts will dictate your actions and manifest your reality. Negative thoughts can kill dreams, while positive thoughts will ignite your tomorrows. Believe that you were born to do this. What you place in your mind will become your reality. The most important story you'll ever tell is your own. What kind of story are you telling yourself? Make sure it's a good one, because you are listening. What you think, you will become. Our thoughts dictate what comes out of our mouths, so it is important to keep positive and bridle the tongue. Practicing positive thoughts may mean making some adjustments, practicing some mental gymnastics, and retraining our thoughts. It can take changing "the landscape" of people, places, and things in order to create a new, positive environment. You need these elements to stay the course. The more you speak positive words over your life, the more sunny situations you will encounter. "Send your words in the direction you want your life to go," as Joel Osteen so eloquently says. Remember, it all starts with a seed… your thoughts. Water and nurture your thoughts. Practice makes perfect. Try it and watch the transformation.

Our thoughts create our words, which will manifest our world. Your words are powerful, so speak and tell your story with a happy ending. You can't talk negativity and expect positivity. Remind yourself daily… I CAN, I Will, I AM ENOUGH. You want it? Whatever it is, whether personally or professionally, we have a lot more power than we know to manifest goodness, abundance, and transformation in our lives.

When you shift your thinking and reframe the narrative of your story and share it with the world differently, everything changes. It all starts and ends with us. We have more power than we know. When our thoughts and actions are in alignment, they create consistency. They'll shape what we say and do in this world. We talk the talk and walk the walk. Claim it and walk in the hope and confidence like you already own it.

#IDAREYOU

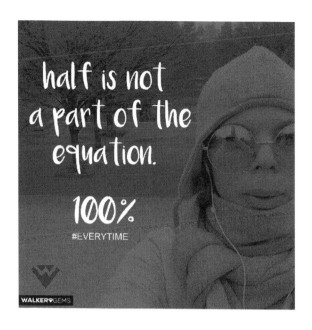

COMPETENCE
CONFIDENCE
CLARITY

COMPETENCE

Success is peace of mind, which is a direct result of self-satisfaction in knowing you did your best to become the best you are capable of becoming. —John Wooden

You would never leave your house to go somewhere without the directions for your destination, but many of us actually go through our lives like that...we're lost. We plan for our careers, for vacations, for college, for parties, for celebrations, but many of us don't have a plan for our lives. What if you decided to run the NYC Marathon, a total of 25 miles, but never trained a day in your life before the race? You live in Kansas and took a NYC flight the day before the race, never bothered to understand the rules or where the start and end destination are located. Honestly, that's what a lot of people do with their lives. We find ourselves in this life with ideas and passions, but we fail to ever investigate, research, plan, and take action. We become drifters without a plan. Having a dream and realizing our dream are two different things. Have a vision. Create a plan. Network. Find bridges of hope. There is an overload of information out there. Find relevant organizations, conferences, or seminars for your networking and continued education.

Edx.org—Founded by MIT and Harvard University in 2012, this learning platform offers high-powered courses from the world's best universities to all.

Meetup.com—Good resource to connect and figure out your #tribevibe.

#The3Cs

CONFIDENCE

Stand tall, be humble, and act like you're supposed to be "in the room." You attract what you're expecting. Confidence of self is a key ingredient and shows up in the image that we project to the world. It sets the tone for who we are and how we think about ourselves. What do you want your first impression to be? Remember, energy is contagious. Don't let the fear of making wrong decisions hold you back from making a decision. Confidence is key and we all have to make daily decisions, and we all make mistakes, but the trick is to learn from them, bounce back, and press forward. Not taking action can be more costly than a mistake, because when you do something and make a mistake, at least there is movement and you're learning. Taking no action is like watching your ship sink.

There's a myth that confidence and humility can't co-exist. We're divine creatures that are here to radiate light, stand in hope, and strut our stuff. This includes our posture, a proper handshake, good eye contact, and making sure that people can hear us when we speak. If you're not strong with these qualities, start practicing this behavior daily. It will eventually become natural with habitual repetition. The first step is to acknowledge any areas for improvement. Believe in yourself, and then the rest of the world will believe in you. From there, all possibilities flow.

As a leader, your confidence is everything. These five factors will build your confidence muscles:
1. Being emotionally fit
2. Being psychologically strong
3. Being physically fit
4. Being spiritually grounded
5. Being evolutionary

CLARITY.

Make your vision crystal clear. I love to visualize my destination and allow myself the space to paint the picture and envision. What God planted inside of you, that special sauce that you have inside, no one else can take or re-create, because it's only for you. You are the originator and not the imitator with your purpose. Once you claim it, move forward and work on crafting it. A purpose-filled life has obstacles and challenges, but the road is worth it to travel. At the times in my life when I've been focused, and in alignment with my purpose, I've found peace in the midst of the storm. I am here to serve, empower others, and act as a conduit. In hindsight, it's the times in my life when there was a lack of clarity that I felt a lot of resistance, a lack of peace in the midst of the storms, and it was also where I digressed and was sidetracked by easy distractions. There was no focus.

Get crystal clear about what you want to achieve and what your perfect world is.

1. Paint the picture…with detail. Don't leave a thing out.

2. Now, you need to make a list of resources, people, places, tools, apps, and whatever can support this picture and bring it to life.

3. After brainstorming, organize it in an outline… stage 1, 2, 3, etc.

4. Now grab a calendar and create an immediate, actionable timeline from your outline with small steps.

5. I don't like to create more than three to five big goals within a three- to six-month period. Take it in stages.

6. In order to eat, you need to learn how to fish. Google reputable and valuable podcasts, blogs, and webinars that spotlight your subject. Follow them. You have to know how to find, engage, and focus on people that make sense and fit your brand and services and that share your vision.

7. Learn how to cultivate tribe members using hashtags and searches that are in alignment with your subject, finding social groups of the same lifestyle.

8. Make sure to accomplish least one intimidating action toward your long-term plan daily.

Live an intentional life. Set your own calendar, blueprint, and plan. This includes self-preservation time like working out, prayer, and taking the time to do the things that keep you in balance for life and the long haul. The clearer and more specific you are with your dreams and goals, the more tangible they become. Here's the thing: In order to achieve, you have to get up off of that couch and stop telling people what you want to do and start doing it. Trust that you will make mistakes, but once you start, you'll discover the universe will be there to support your passion.

DAILY DEPOSITS GIVE THE BEST RETURN ON INVESTMENT (ROI)

What are your daily deposits? 40, 60, 80, or 100%? Dreams aren't realized by clicking our heels, and there are no overnight success stories. Your private practice will dictate your public performance. A series of small choices over time with consistency will produce dramatic results. If consistent water streaming daily over time can alter the character of land or change the shape of rocks, imagine how consistent behavior over time can change your life! The best ROI comes from applying daily deposits of faith, sweat equity, tenacity, and understanding. In time, these will yield a great return. This sounds so simple, but it really takes consistent practice to instill these small changes daily, which can lead to big changes that ultimately can change the trajectory of our lives forever from our health to our relationships to our finances to our business to our peace. This may take some reconfiguring or retraining in our practices, habits, and disciplines to achieving the results.

You have to get to first base before you get the home run. There is only one way to get to the top of the mountain, and that's by climbing it, one step at a time, with upward mobility. Before you can enjoy the fruit, you have to focus on the root.

Consistency is built on steady practices that form habits. It's challenging. There will be many days when you just don't feel like it, especially when you're trying to do something positive like stick to a diet, exercise, or drill through your day. When you're YOUR own boss, you may not always feel like plowing through the challenges in front of you.

Doing the things that most won't do on a regular basis is what separates the leaders from the masses and greatness from mediocrity. Nothing will ever become great without hard work, leveling up and working out the pain points. These are the times we find out how badly we want it. They create the stories and memories of the days you stuck to it and in your consistency and resiliency, somehow you woke up one day and were GREAT. That's what those "overnight success" ten-year-plus stories are all about.

People always speak about Jay Z and his mega success story, but what many don't know is that before anyone knew about Jay's music, he was crafting his skills. Since his teens, he was working on his music, trying to find the right record label, knocking on countless doors for at least ten years before he had his first big hit. He stayed focused and didn't give up, and eventually started his own thing, and that's when things fell in place. He never took no for an answer and always stayed true to his vision. Jay Z believed in himself. Often, the things we want to do the least are the things we need to do the most. I've noticed that big wins come from taking a series of small steps in the right direction. Keep your eye on the prize.

When I started my first business called Fashion in Effect, a custom tailor shop in Brooklyn, I was 21. I had no business experience except for my hustle. I had an idea, a shoestring budget, and a lot of faith that it could happen. I learned about this business by hands-on experience. I built trust in my community by engaging with the customers.

I had a consistent seven-day-a-week work ethic and invested daily deposits of my sweat equity, honing my skills, building relationships, and gaining a customer base. What people don't realize is that for the first three years of my business, I became so familiar with beans and rice dinners, and many sleepless nights, because I was also making daily financial deposits in my business that required sacrifices. I had to miss out on social events with friends, eating steak dinners, and vacations. The tradeoff was definitely worth it. There isn't a university in the world that could teach me better than my real-life experience. I have a rich inside-out experience.

My deposits eventually gave me an ROI that allowed me to travel the world, meet some of the most interesting folks, work with legends, live my dreams, and create a self-sustaining income that has allowed me many blessings. Sometimes I look back and say, "Did that really happen?" I'm in awe. I've come a long way from that young girl in Clinton Hill, Brooklyn, to traveling the world in pursuit of my dreams. You just keep chipping away, and watch—your blessings will eventually rain down on you.

#keepchippingaway

#dontstopgetitit

you have
what it takes

#believe

WALKER♥GEMS

**Discipline is the bridge
 between thought and accomplishment.**

—A.R. Bernard

CONSISTENCY TRANSFORMS INTO DISCIPLINE THAT CREATES CONGRUENCY IN YOUR LIFE THAT WILL ALLOW FREEDOM.

There is no such thing as microwave success. I wish it was as easy as ordering fast food, but the reality is it takes years of daily disciplines and constant practice to become the likes of a Nadia Lopez, Tim Ferriss, Lisa Nichols, Oprah Winfrey, Magic Johnson, or Barbara Corcoran. Greatness is not something that we are. It's something we do…over and over and over again on purpose until we become. Repetition is everything. It's important to train your thoughts and move your actions forward. The more efficient we are, the closer we move towards our future goals. Set up repetitious, actionable, and definable goals and enable them. Be intentional. Once you become committed to the process, positive changes occur. It's inside-out changes. Your life really can become somewhat of automated pilot system that works for you.

I'm a constant work in progress because my creative tank is always competing with my think tank.. I've noticed that whenever I've made changes and implemented new automated systems with consistent habits, and practiced them, there is always a lot less stress with better productivity.

Gretchen Rubin offers an interesting perspective for small and big changes and developing habits and discipline in "The Happiness Project." As she eloquently states, "The days are long but the years are short."

Discipline will allow freedom in your life. Consistency over time will create congruency and wins that translate into your personal and professional life.

DISCERNMENT

It is not a daily increase, but a daily decrease. Hack away at the inessentials.

—Bruce Lee

The more discernment you display, the more clarity will show up. Discernment helps your decision-making skills. Knowing what we want and why we want it, helps us in shaping the right disciplines in our life. I've found for myself, a lot of times the things I wanted may have brought me immediate gratification, a sense of temporary security, a feel-good factor, or an ego boost, but the effects for my long-term well-being were not the same. I know you've heard, what feels good is not always good for you. In a different way, when we don't want to do something, sometimes that's absolutely the thing that we should be doing—like working out. Think about this when applying discernment and discipline to the decision-making process in your life.

Consider the compound effect. If you always have a knee-jerk reaction concerning your wants and needs, you're not in control. Your long-term view is out of focus, and it's easier to encounter setbacks.

Our "wants" usually don't pair well with discipline and consistency. You have to set boundaries and stick to change. If you have a business but don't operate on a budget and don't adhere to the plan, and you make irresponsible or impromptu financial decisions, that will yield counterproductive outcomes.

Obey your goals by respecting them, applying discipline, and discerning "wants vs. needs." Before one can grow and sustain or manage big things, we need to be able to remain faithful and be consistent in the small things. It's about incremental gains.

Decisions shape destiny. —Tony Robbins

Three Actionable Step Questions

What do you want to do?

Example: I want to exercise three times a week on Monday, Wednesday, and Friday at 6 a.m. for 30 minutes.

Why?

Example: I want to have a healthy lifestyle, so I can have more energy for my children, because I want to live longer and feel good or set an example for my family.

Identify three actionable steps you can take. Here are some examples:

I will start saving $_____ amount every Friday.

I'll work out at 8AM on Wednesdays for 60 min.

I commit to investing in my self-development for 3 hours every week on Fridays and Saturdays.

Now, when? With a calendar, write down what you want to do, why, and the days and times you commit to doing these things.

_____

_____

_____

_____

_____

_____

_____

PASSION

+

PURPOSE

Purpose and passion will lead you to profit. My definition of profit is a robust experience that encapsulates happiness, fulfillment, peace, and monetary gains that result in a #richinsideout experience.

So often people are working hard at the wrong thing. Working on the right thing is probably more important than working hard.

—Caterina Fake, cofounder of Flickr

When your vision and purpose are stronger than your ability to withstand rejection, you will see your dreams be realized—it will happen. You will be unstoppable. If you think about something all the time and dream about it, from the time you wake up to the time you go to bed, then that's your passion. Passion will fuel you and lead you to your purpose. Pursue your passion. Life is too short not to pursue what you love. If you find out what you're passionate about, investigate it. Maybe you love clothes and you put your outfits together and you get compliments all the time when you go out without even trying. If that's you, it might be worth it to check out the fashion industry and all the career possibilities. You could be a fashion stylist, a visual merchandiser, a buyer, blogger, fashion designer, or maybe you're an influencer. You may love books. You can't stop reading and you enjoy writing. Entertain having your own blog or being a writer or a book critic, working as an editor…there are so many choices, branches to the foundation of your subject of interest.

There is a fulfillment and peace when you're sowing seeds and utilizing your God-given gifts…those unique abilities that no one has like you do! Yes, there may be 10,000,00 others that do the same things you do, but not like you do them and not with your magic sauce. If you know you have it, you need to tap into those things you're better at than others without trying. A lot of times our gift is also the thing we most ignore, run from, or refuse to recognize. Why?

We think finding our passion has to be more difficult. It doesn't. We all have something unique to offer the world.

The profit will be a residual from your passion with purpose. It is a match made in heaven. You will find that doors will open and "when you commit to it, the world will assist to it." Profit is a full-circle experience. Your profit will include your happiness, purpose, passion, peace, and financial gain, all rolled up in a well-rounded experience that will make you #richinsideout.

#passionoverprofit

BET ON YOU

God doesn't require us to succeed, he only requires that you try.

—Mother Teresa

Guy Routte, who is a veteran in the entertainment industry and a dear friend whom I trust and have the privilege of working with, once told me this story that stuck with me. In Guy's own words...

"When I was 19 years old, I had a job as a customer service representative at Municipal Credit Union. It was a really good-paying job for a kid and the environment was friendly, and I was really good at this job. I excelled because I cared about the customer and empathized with their problems and committed myself to finding solutions.

"One day at the job, for various reasons, I decided I no longer wanted to work there. Actually, I didn't want to work anywhere for anyone. I wanted to forge my own path. I wanted a life in the entertainment business, music specifically.

Without much thought I approached my supervisor and informed her that this would be my final day on the job. Surprised and not sure how to respond, she simply said OK. I returned to my seat to finish the day. A bit later in the day the supervisor told me my presence was requested with the president of MCU. I'd never been to that floor or to his office and only met him a few times in passing. I went in and he asked me why I was leaving. I told him that music was my passion and I needed to seriously work at it and this was taking time and energy away from that pursuit. He said he understood but he asked me to give him two weeks notice. He informed me that this is customary for anyone quitting their job.

"Confused (this was my first real job so I'd never heard of that rule), I asked, 'If you fired me would you give me two weeks notice?' He laughed and said no, that's not how it works. You give two weeks so that if you need a recommendation for your next job you can get one because you left this job in good standing. Ahhh, I said, well, not to worry, I'm never working for anyone again, so no referral needed. I'm done today. He said, OK, I'll give you 30 days to change your mind, shook my hand, and that was it. I never changed my mind and almost 30 years later I have not worked for anyone.

"I have my own company, and although it's been up and down, I don't regret a moment and I don't regret not giving him those two weeks. That was my message to the universe that I was serious about the direction I was headed and I had faith that if I walk my path sincerely, the universe would conspire on my behalf to protect me and guide me and bring me success.

"One of the greatest decisions I've ever made."

—Guy Routte, War Media

Why shouldn't you bet on yourself? No one can do a better YOU than YOU. You know what you're capable of. You know what works for you and what doesn't. You can manage your weaknesses and focus on your strengths. With supreme willpower, laser focus, and a relentless belief system, you can move mountains once you get going.

No one is going to be a better *coach, student, and cheerleader* than you can be to yourself. At the same time, you can be your worst enemy, so be careful where and how you choose to place your energy. Energy grows. We cannot conquer the world until we conquer ourselves.

#BYOB

BE YOUR OWN BRAND

All of us need to understand the importance of branding. We are CEOs of our own companies: Me Inc. To be in business today, our most important job is to be head marketer for the brand called YOU.

—Tom Peters in Fast Company

Your vision now and your vision over time will change and grow, just as our world is everchanging. Technology has brought a new way of thinking and gives us all a fair shot. Social selling has become very important. Google is the number one way to achieve sales on the Internet, followed by Facebook ads. We are always Googling, researching, reading reviews, and tagging people whenever we see something that we like. We've experienced a serious new technological transformation.

There are 30 million of us working from home at least once a week. We've become better negotiators, and we're changing the way we choose to handle our business. We are all in the business of BYOB (Be Your Own Brand). You will get what you negotiate, not what you're worth.

The fact is, how you represent yourself counts, whether you are working within a small business, a major corporation, have your own company, or consider yourself a freelancer. Positioning your brand to be in alignment with your value system and what your brand represents is important. From your messaging to your aesthetic to your lifestyle to your #wgtribevibe to your community, your positioning should be consistent. Consistently hone your skills in order to increase your brand worth and BYOB.

I've watched leaders become great by constantly learning, evolving, honing their skills, serving others and offering value, and networking with like-minded folks who will help them stand tall. Read incessantly and continue your education via classes, certifications, and so on. I am also a big fan of podcasts and discovering new things through online resources. I have a lot of virtual mentors who inspire me as well.

Whether it's you personally, or you being an extension of your brand, be your own brand, at all times, especially living in this digital era.

DISPEL THE
FOLLOWING
MYTHS

#1. We all have to be number one. We don't. It's not real. That's why there's number two, number five, and number 10,003. Life is more interesting with variety. This is important to remember and recognize—that you can find your passion, live a purpose-filled life, offer service to the world, and have an abundant and #richinsideout life if you are any number.

#2. You need a hero. Don't wait to find a hero. That's too much responsibility for one person. You need to be your own hero.

#3. I'm not good with money or I can't save. Yes, you can. Learn to create healthy habits from the start. Start small and build up from there. Here's a link to getting started with some basics:

http://money.cnn.com/pf/money-essentials

#4. Don't believe you have to defer your dreams. "When the kids leave the house, I will start working on my dream." You may have said that you have to wait until you have the perfect plan, have it all figured out, or you aren't afraid. There's never a perfect time, but there is always a way to make it happen. Tomorrow is not promised, so if you need to transition into your dream slowly, start. Set a plan, make smart and calculated moves, but make moves. If you have a job, either wake up an hour or two earlier or come home, tuck the kids in, and stay up an extra hour or two investing in your dream.

#5. I can't. They're smarter. There is a big chance that this is NOT true. Even if so, this does not mean that you are not worthy of success. Success is largely a result of consistent behavior, with a process that produces results over time. It's the product of ordinary people who do the extraordinary work daily. It's doing what most won't do.

#6. You have to be mean to win and be respected. I've found people are motivated when they're happy and can feel the love. The more you serve and lift up people and celebrate them, the more you will ignite contagious behavior. What kind of culture are you creating? Your external world will be an extension of your internal culture.

#7. If I'm doing what I love, success will come easy to me. Nothing worth it is easy all of the time. Whether you tap into your passion or have a job that you hate, it is going to be work. Success comes with constant upgrades, smart applications, elbow grease, and hustle with muscle. There is no way around the work; however, following your passion is the difference between loving or hating what you do daily.

#8. Fronting. "Ain't no future in fronting." The truth always comes to light. If you have a whole bunch of fake followers, or if you're living beyond your means just to impress others, if you have hype but there is no substance, eventually the truth will come to light. You want an authentic experience.

#9. I don't need to work on self-development, honing my skills in order to go the distance. If you don't, you'll hit a ceiling. It's like making a cake and taking it out of the oven too soon. The cake sinks and deflates.

#10. Find mentors and business coaches, or even virtual mentors in the areas that you want to grow. Welcome reverse mentorship. We can learn a lot from younger people, just as they can learn from us.

SET

WELCOME TO THE DISCOMFORT ZONE.

The ultimate measure of a man is not where he stands in the moments of comfort and convenience, but where he stands at times of challenge and controversy.

—Martin Luther King.

Change is the one constant element in life, but it's the one thing we fight the most. Successful people learn to adapt to change and push through it. Change is where the magic happens and where we find that next level of growth. It's never easy, but if you want to be a successful entrepreneur or have a better human experience, you need to be ready for it. Be adaptable. When we become a friend to change, we welcome growth. Decide to do the necessary work to become the master of your life to help you reach new horizons. There is a metamorphosis that needs to takes place. When you want to change your body, you have to show up, be committed, be willing to work hard, be sore. Most often, in the daily grind, it's hard to see the results, especially in the beginning. You can be diligent, sweating up a storm, pushing yourself past your "limits," and you look in the mirror or jump on the scale and say, when am I going to meet my goal? When am I going to be able to see it? It's not visible to us. We can feel so fatigued that we don't feel like we can do that last rep or run that last mile. We feel like we are going to die and pass out, but when we push past the pain, fatigue, doubt, and voices in our heads, we finish strong. When we stay committed to this stubborn, consistent behavior, change and transformation show up.

The same is true of your life or business. If you have your eyes fixed on a goal, stay committed and don't give up, especially when you're in that muddy middle. Put those rain boots on and trudge through it. Eventually you will see your transformation. Think of it as enrolling yourself in the boot camp of life. Embrace the discomfort zone necessary to change the course of your life.

action over comfort

WALKER♥GEMS

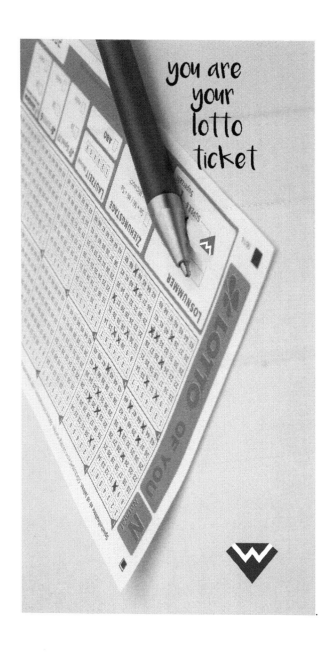

DREAMS AREN'T REALIZED WITHOUT CHOPPING THAT WOOD DAILY.

#chopthatwood
#hustlewithmuscle
#cantstopwontstop

DO YOUR HOMEWORK

Most of us are foodies. We love food. What if you were in a restaurant and saw that your neighbor was served a beautiful dish that looked amazing? You were sold on ordering the same thing without checking out the ingredients or asking questions. You didn't have any details, but you ordered it anyway. After you ordered it and it came to the table, it was so good and you pulled out your phone and took a picture and posted it on Instagram with a caption that said #yougottaeatthis. Finally, you taste it. It has peanuts in it, and you're allergic to them. You get an allergic reaction and break out in hives. It's a buzz killer—honestly, what looked so good turned out to be a downright nasty experience.

Don't order something you're going to hate. Do your homework and research the subject first before sinking your teeth into it and becoming disappointed. A lot of us romanticize what we think we want to pursue without doing enough research on the field. For instance, so many people think they want to be in fashion until they understand the grind behind it. Many become disillusioned when they actually start doing the work. The same is true of entrepreneurship. It's become the hype and the new buzzword. Everyone wants to sign up to be an entrepreneur without recognizing that it takes a special DNA. Don't do it for the accolades, because it's a thankless job. You must have a relentless passion for it, an inconceivable work ethic, a huge conviction to serve, and a willpower and determination like no other.

If you've done your homework and you're still convinced that you really want to pursue your passion, then study and follow the patterns of successful people in your lane. Find out their behavior, habits, routines, down to their reading list. Check out their lifestyle, follow their podcasts, go to their conferences, read their books, and take notes from their failures and successes. Get jewels from proven models.

Don't follow advice from people who have no track record or that you wouldn't want to trade places with.

Behavior is key. Most successful people have some common essentials such as early rising (before 7AM), working out as a part of their lifestyle, creating other healthy habits. They're big on serving others but value their time and develop dream teams. They are constantly students. They also surround themselves with others who make them better, from coaches to mentors to therapists to teammates and tribe members that play an integral part in building the vision.

WALKERGEMS

There are so many books great reads for entrepreneurs Here are few good ones to check out.

1. The Compound Effect, by Darren Hardy

2. Start With Why, by Simon Sinek

3. The 7 Habits of Highly Effective People, by Stephen R. Covey

4. Intentional Living: Choosing a Life That Matters, by John Maxwell

There are tons of others, but these are great for anyone. I suggest you do your own research and make a list of others to stretch your growth and be obsessive about it.

April Walker

The only thing that relieves pressure is preparation.

—Tom Kite

A big part of the equation is preparation. If we have a great idea, then we can't forget the most important component. Below are realistic questions aimed at startups or individuals with ideas for businesses or brands to help you figure out how you are going to grow your baby. Some of these are relevant across the board when planning any project. Many of us are visual thinkers, and we grasp ideas much better when we can see them in drawings.

Feel free to customize and develop your own questions. This serves as a template or guideline for inspiration to get your wheels spinning.

How we are going to get there?

What's the feasibility of it?

What are the risks associated with it?

What is the financial investment? What are the costs to absorb?

Who is my competition?

What kind of margins will I have?

What kind of automated systems do I need to create in order to minimize my heavy lifting and downsize stress?

Who are my potential customers?

What is their social profile (psychographics, demographics)?

How will I find them and reach them? How will I market to them?

What will my work ethic need to be like to sustain this kind of business? Am I built for the kind of sweat equity this dream will require?

How will my day change with this blueprint?

How will my life change as a result of this vision?

NOTES:

_____

_____

_____

_____

_____

_____

_____

_____

_____

_____

_____

_____

_____

_____

_____

_____

_____

_____

_____

_____

_____

_____

When you're first thinking through an idea, it's important not to get bogged down in complexity. Thinking simply and clearly is hard to do.

—Richard Branson, founder of Virgin Group

DON'T OVERPLAN.

Newsflash. Your plan will look good on paper, but I guarantee it will change. Check this out…it was discovered that that only twelve percent of the founders of Inc. 500 companies conducted formal market research before their launch and forty percent wrote business plans, according to a 2002 survey, and of those that wrote plans, two-thirds of them admitted they got rid of them later."

We're living in the most exciting and ever-changing time of history. We're participants in a technology era that's changing the way we learn, the way we communicate, and the way we do business. Business practices, and the way we interact with our audiences, continue to change at a phenomenal rate. The factors that were once the most important considerations are no more.

Can you imagine that we actually frequented stores and listened to music in the record stores? If you're a millennial, you may have missed out. CDs and DVDs are becoming a thing of the past. Now we have downloads on iTunes. Remember the door-to-door salesman?

No one does, because they're just about extinct. We purchase online or from our phone.

The Internet has also made it easier to find money for your ideas through services such as Circle Up, Kiva, and so many more. We all have access to connect and engage with celebrities and influencers directly through social media.

Everything is changing so fast that you have to build a fluid plan. There was a time when it was taboo not to have a three- to five-year plan with projections and numbers, a very detailed plan. I don't believe in this anymore. Projections and numbers are good for goal setting, and still necessary if you're presenting to investors, but rarely are they a match to the reality once you start doing.

Today, planning at length is futile because while you're spending time over-researching and micromanaging your perfect plan, someone else has started doing and grabbing your potential customers. I believe that starting out with a fluid, visionary plan with a guideline blueprint is essential, but understand that you'll need to tweak, revisit, and potentially change your plan once you get started. If you're paying attention, you'll understand over time what your tribe members want and discover how to serve them better. Be like more like water and less like a rock. You need to be nimble and agile in today's world as you BYOB.

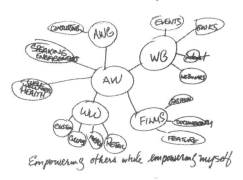

It's not because I'm smarter but I hustle harder, and that makes me unstoppable.

#beunstoppable

There is no microwave success formula. It takes #hustlewithmuscle, a lot of heart, and sweat equity. There's no way around hard work. I don't care what course you take and what pill you decide to pop, if you want it, you have to work for it. There's no circumventing doing the work. There must be sacrifice for the gain.

People never see the grind or the hustle. The fact is that entrepreneurs have a different life. If you're in the fashion or entertainment business, the hype is perceived as even more glamorous. It's an illusion. They don't know that 99 percent of the time, there is a commitment to work later and longer hours, network on the days you may not feel like it, and live a CRAZY GRIND. That runway snapshot is one percent of the whole picture. I'm sure it's like that in every other industry. Don't judge a book by its cover. To be your own boss, you have to be unstoppable with tough skin. You have to hustle harder and make the days count. Don't wait for the opportunity; create the opportunity. You can't be on cruise control when you're passionate about your dreams. Set your plan to go after audacious goals daily, and focus on the big dream, attacking it in small achievable bites.

There is no clicking your heels. If you want it, you have to go get it, without complaint, but instead with humility, determination, confidence, and gratitude. Success comes in time, with repeated and consistent small efforts that add up. Invest with sweat equity, be persistent and stay determined. It's mandatory to the success of your journey. You can only get to the top of a mountain by climbing. Dreams don't become real, and the vision doesn't get executed, without taking the steps and doing the work. The biggest thing about successful people is that they're doing the things that most people won't do. They're working while most are sleeping. You have to want it as much as you want to sleep and eat.

#UEatWhatUKill

People think the grass is greener on the other side – well, guess what, it is for some.

We all get the same seeds, but we have to plant them, water, cultivate them, and nourish them to grow. Get your green thumb on. This is how you change your reality. I've found my biggest opportunities were created—they didn't fall in my lap.

When I relaunched my fashion brand Walker Wear, everyone didn't understand my decision to do an exclusive online e-commerce shop and market my personal brand via a social media strategy, because when I originally launched, my prior distribution outlets were department stores, chains, and boutiques, and honestly, that's the way many fashion brands distribute their goods.

With my new model, I've connected with my #wwtribevibe and have been so thankful to amplify our Walker Wear brand and messaging, garnering our global presence. Because of this Internet connection and amplification, I've procured some amazing opportunities such as being featured in the Huffington Post, on several podcasts, in an American Express Open Forum and a Ford Escape commercial, and included in a Brooklyn Museum Sneaker Exhibition, plus so many other opportunities. If I never jumped in and picked up my own bullhorn and started sharing my story (without a publicist), I might still be waiting for an opportunity. I would be waiting for press, and my consumers wouldn't know about me.

If somebody told me twenty years ago that this would happen, I would've thought they were crazy, yet, it's really possible. You can write your own ticket, create your own dream job, be your own boss, or choose to keep a job and be a side-gigger with a part-time hustle. Your present job may facilitate your investment for your future dream business. Whatever it is, with a little ingenuity, imagine what outcome you wish to have, and you can always reverse engineer.

#HUSTLEWITHMUSCLE

Studies show that people who exercise over years and years have bigger brains.

In order to be your best, you have to feel your best. I firmly believe that your physical being affects your mental state. We think how we feel, and how we feel affects our overall state. When you work out, your body actually releases endorphins that help reduce stress, and the increase of the BDNF proteins in our brains acts as a mood enhancer that increases our level of happiness as well. A healthy physical state enhances a healthy mind.

It builds confidence in your character, and these consistent practices serve as an aid of discipline on your path to success. Remember you have to #hustlewithmuscle to be equipped to carry your dreams daily. Can you believe that you could gain a bigger brain from exercising consistently over the years? You want your physical, mental, and spiritual abilities to work in tandem. The results in a robust vertical human optimization experience." It's about alignment and congruency for your mind, body, and soul. You want to be able to physically carry your dreams and go the distance.

#HealthisWealth: Set a weekly exercise calendar. First write down specific routines you will do, whether it's walking, running, weight training, or yoga. Now write down the days and times you will commit to doing the work with specificity.

my workout schedule

SUNDAY	MONDAY	TUESDAY	WEDNESDAY	THURSDAY	FRIDAY	SATURDAY
rest	yoga	stairs	abs weights	stairs	interval training	prospect park

Failure is never fatal; it's the down payment you pay for success.

—Dennis Kimbro

#theFword

FAILURE

First things first...we need to address FAILURE...that word that no one ever wants to include in their vocabulary. Yet it's one of those things we all have in common. We've all experienced failure. In fact, nearly half of all marriages end in divorce these days, and almost all of our New Year's resolutions end up failing. Though the "F" word is taboo, it's an inevitable thing that happens to us all in this lifetime, and we encounter it more than "success." It is the one word that has a lot of power. We need to #RESPECT it. It can break our spirits and make us feel defeated or like losers. When we change the way we think about failure, addressing it and dealing with it and the feelings associated with it, failure can actually be useful.

Here's the thing—from the time we're born, we learn that failure is something really negative, with adverse effects, penalties, embarrassment, alienation, and a lot more. Honestly, no one likes to embrace it, but I want to offer food for thought.

Think about folding failure into your narrative and staying honest about it. Welcome the confrontation, analyzing your experiences and learning from them. Allow that "F" word to propel you to your next opportunity. Fail forward. There is always a lesson in failure that teaches us something we need to grow. When we do introspective work, we get the lesson. It makes us stronger, more prepared, and once we go through it, we grow through it, and we become the seasoned experts.

WALKERGEMS

Failure keeps our feet on solid ground. See where the kryptonite is. Why did it affect you in that way? What can you do to deactivate the kryptonite and take away its power? It's like the first time you fell and scraped your knees and saw a little blood and panicked, but you got back up and you kept moving. Real winners know how to take falls, can handle bumps and bruises, and will go the distance. Never give up but shoot with aim and strive to be better, recover, and learn from the mistakes. It takes a lot of vision, faith, gumption, grit, resilience, and perseverance. Know that "I can do this" and walk that walk. Go out there and make it happen. Failure is only failure when you stop trying.

FIVE GREAT FAILURE STORIES

1. Can you believe that before Walt Disney Films the visionary was fired by a newspaper editor and told HE lacked imagination and had no good ideas? After, he was able to raise $15,000 for his first company called Laugh-O-Gram Films but was eventually forced to close Laugh-O-Gram.

2. Oprah was fired from her first anchor television gig in Baltimore. Imagine that.

3. One of Mr. George Steinbrenner's first sports investments was with the Cleveland Pipers, a small basketball team. The franchise went bankrupt under Steinbrenner's direction in the 1960's (prior to his acquiring the New York Yankees.

4. After Milton Hershey decided he didn't want to work for someone else, he started three candy-related companies that failed before he reached success with his Lancaster Caramel Company and Hershey Company

5. Colonel Harland David Sanders and his famous secret recipe was rejected over 1,000 times before a restaurant finally added it to the menu.

See the possibilities when everyone else is studying the problem. Don't go through it but grow through it. My worst moments have prepared me for my best triumphs. My failures have been connected to my success stories and taught me the most valuable lessons. It's all been part of the journey. Failures are like stepping-stones. Failure doesn't kill us. Our falls provide context for what we might do differently and often promote new possibilities, because we can always see with more clarity in hindsight. There is always a chance to learn if we're paying attention. The lessons I've learned have served me well. If you're not present, you're probably not getting the life lessons, and studying everything else but the lesson at hand. It's much easier to place blame, find fault, or make some excuses. This kind of behavior will stunt your growth. Growth means you're willing to be humble enough to reflect on the experience and accountable enough to own your part and learn from your mistakes. If we don't look in the mirror, we'll keep repeating the same behavior, spinning our wheels, and going nowhere fast.

Since we spend a lifetime becoming acquainted with failures, why not stop running from failure and find out how to make it work for us? This way we can appreciate our journey a lot more. Just like flying, gravity is this force in opposition, but when you respect it and understand how it works, it is possible to fly...maybe not the first, second, or third time out, as the Wright Brothers proved to us, but eventually. #FailurecanleadtoFlying

Since failure's inevitable, use it as a strategic resource for growth and take it from the negative to the positive. It's powerful when we soak up each lesson and apply it to the future. Reflecting is a big part of this stage. What we want and what we're ready for can be two different things. Weathering the storms and soaking up the sunshine will prepare you for that big WAVE coming your way.

I failed over and over again in life. That's why I succeed.

—Michael Jordan

Analyze. Acknowledge. Write down obstacles or things that keep you weighed down from moving forward. Knock them down one by one. You may need to develop new, enriching relationships or acknowledge that you need to scale back spending in order to save money for a "dream account."

For example, you hit a brick wall, you hit a point where you are having a problem, or maybe your best sales agent broke out or you may have invested major dollars into products you just knew would sell but they are now sitting in the warehouse and are collecting dust because you couldn't move them. At some point, we all are going to have our own failures, woes, and disappointments. Accept where you are and what went wrong. They say it's not how many times you get knocked down but how many times you get up. We're going to fall on our butts. It hurts and we feel defeated, but shake it off. While we can acknowledge the pain point, we can't stay there. More time and energy need to be spent on creating the solution, and finding a resolution. Understand that your present moment is the result of choices you've made in your past, but that doesn't mean that your today has to define your tomorrow. We can change the trajectory of our lives, but in order to change it, you may need to:

BREAK GLASS
IN CASE
OF EMERGENCY

Entrepreneurs are going to have these three qualities rolled up in one. GUTS, GRIT, and GUMPTION. In order to be our best, we have to be able to take responsibility for our mistakes and shortcomings, and be forgiving to ourselves. One of my life lessons was when I bought a home in the country and had plans to have a retreat and a peaceful sanctuary on the weekends. It was a great plan, but a few things happened. I invested in a pet business simultaneously and was working long hours, so I wasn't able to enjoy the home enough. Also, my pet shop wasn't bringing in money fast enough, and I had invested in the stock market. The stock market crashed and I took a big hit. On top of that, I saw the real estate market getting ready to plunge because of the whole subprime-lending situation taking place. I made an assessment and knew that I needed to sell because all of it was too much to maintain or I would lose it all. I needed to lighten my load. I bought the country home as an investment. I was able to recoup my investment, but it was still a very hard decision. I felt like a failure, but I didn't want to lose even more money. Sometimes you have to make hard decisions that will make you feel like a failure. Always take the emotion out of your decisions and look at the facts. Failure can serve great lessons.

We should always draw from our experiences, and identify and reflect on what went wrong and how we can grow from them. In hindsight, I bit off more than I could chew at once. Still, I am thankful that I was able to assess and exercise damage control.

Fear of failure and being ignorant of the facts are inhibitors to our growth. Ignoring the pain points and becoming paralyzed by fear doesn't help us. When these factors set in, most people drop out of the race. They built up mountains in their heads that obstruct the light, creative energy, and possibilities. You'll need GUTS to move forward, and with GRIT, take the bull by the horns, riding it out with a little bit of crazy. With GUMPTION, strength, and your special mojo sauce, you'll build resilience muscles. These are necessary traits to live as an entrepreneur. Forge forward.

#TripleGStatus

I have not failed. I've just found 10,000 ways that won't work. —Thomas Edison, inventor of the electric lightbulb

Think of your growth in levels and stages.

It's like an outline. Don't look at trying to achieve everything at once or take on the whole thing at once, because that's overwhelming. Take it one step at a time, master each stage, and before you know it, you've taken yourself from the first stage and you've become a master. Also, when you take this approach, you'll recover from your mistakes with more damage control.

April Walker

SEVEN GOLDEN GEMS

#hustlewithmuscle and have balance. Without our health, success doesn't mean a thing.

#pause Take time to just "be." Sometimes we can be "so busy being busy" that we forget to breathe and take time to replenish ourselves. When you pause and quiet your mind, that's when your ideas will flow. The answers come. It's like replenishing our creative wheel and filling up our tank. According to the Huffington Post, a number of studies show that relaxing protects your heart, lowers your risk of catching a cold, boosts your memory, and lowers your stroke risk. Stress can kill brain cells and double a woman's risk of breast cancer.

#yourspirit We all have our own spiritual connection and faith. I'm not here to judge or dictate, but I will recommend that you spend time connecting. It's good for your soul and if integrated as a way of life, it can give you the best balance for living in this world. I can see the shift in my life since I've started dedicating time daily to my faith, and the difference from practicing mindful meditation with visualization. It centers me, provides me with light, hope, and love and gives me a quiet peace and confidence in the midst of the crazy days. I also can feel and see the difference when I skip a day.

#beyourbestfriend Look in the mirror and fall in love with that person. Discover what it takes to know yourself, like yourself, and love yourself. Discover what your own needs and wants are. What are your interests…what do you enjoy? Be good to yourself and accept yourself as a constant work-in-progress. Honor yourself, and spend time with you. Acknowledge your small wins. They create and lead you to the big ones. When you're good to yourself and treat yourself with the love that you deserve, you're setting a tone for the rest of the world to respect and follow.

#techdetox Challenge! I think it's good to take periodic timeouts. Take a break from your social media once in a while to drown out distractions and instead choose to get centered. They say the average person checks Facebook 14 times a day, and according to Time.com, the average person checks his or her phone 46 times a day. At nighttime, make sure that you're not sleeping with your phone next to your bed. Put it in another room so you have peace where you sleep. You want to have a restful sleep.

#touchsomebody We're living in a digital era. While it's important to be an active participant, it's also important to remember there's a real world out there. Disconnect to connect. There is nothing out there that can replace touch and feel. They say we each should have at least one daily touch. We are in a real deficit. We're spending less and less time with each other and more and more time with our devices. They're replacing our relationships. It's important to integrate the best of both worlds, and to keep perspective on what's really important. #Love #Life #Friends and #FamilyFirst. Friends and family will keep you in check, keep you humble, and tell you the truth. Show me where you spend your time, and I'll show you what you really care about and what's important in your life.

#gratitude It puts it all in perspective. No matter how bad your day gets, remember that you woke up today. Everything else is gravy.

GO

BRAVO! YOU'VE DECIDED TO SEIZE THOSE DREAMS.

You've decided. You have to go for it. In spite of the grind, the commitment you have to make, and the times that you know the checks won't be in the mail and some sleepless nights, you still need to do this. Think of success as a 360-degree experience that's inclusive of fulfillment, productivity, happiness, and monetary compensation. We may not all hit the financial Lotto status, but I've met many millionaires in my life who are unhappy, unfulfilled, lonely, and haunted, while I've met other people who may not be living in a big tax bracket but are really #richinsideout and are really the Lotto winners, because they're living a purpose-filled life and manifesting their dreams. Those people walk with grace and exude gratitude. They understand their mission is to serve others and plant significant seeds while here on this earth.

Whatever you decide, you need to believe in it, because there will be times that your dream will be the only thing carrying you. It's what will get you up and out of bed in the morning when everyone else thinks you're crazy. Most won't understand, so you have to look past the naysayers. It's your dream and no one else's, so don't look for other people to validate your worth or understand your dream. That's your job. If you have the courage to step out on faith, taking the first step is always the hardest part. Once you begin, you will get affirmations, and the stars will start lining up. As you continue your journey, ideas will start to germinate, growing, shaping, and expanding. Understand that you may have to knock on many doors to get the answers you need and realize the dream that you want. Fortune will start falling into your lap when you've activated faith. Bottom line, action cures fear. Once you start, you'll have a sense of urgency, with a belief system that "this is happening" because it's already in motion. It's like Lego blocks—you have to put down one and connect it to the second and continue to build, making each layer strong, until you build this amazing foundation. Don't get it twisted. It takes time and patience, but the world will conspire to assist your God-given ideas and talents.

My friend Reggie Ossé is a great testimony to this truth. Mr. Ossé obtained his Juris Doctor at Georgetown University Law Center, and afterward became an entertainment attorney. He loved music so much and engaging in conversations with these amazing artists and culture creators. He wanted to learn more about them. He knew he couldn't be the only one who felt like this. His vision kept him up at night and he dreamed about it every day. As counsel to some of the most prestigious and famous artists and companies, including P. Diddy and Roc-A-Fella Records, he achieved notable success. Along his journey, something stirred up in Reggie and a new vision manifested.

Eventually, he took a leap of faith and eventually started "The Combat Jack Show" podcast. He walked away from his career as an entertainment attorney and all of the perks that came with it in pursuit of his passion and dream. I'm sure people thought he was crazy. I'm sure there were nights when Reg doubted himself or had to talk himself into continuing the journey. He had to make many sacrifices over the years, but he held steadfast. As a result, his love, passion, and commitment to hone his skills in the podcasting world proved worth it. His podcast has received praise across multiple platforms. He is also cofounded Loud Speakers Network (@LSNpodcasts), a podcast network that houses a host of other hit podcasts. Reg also is now on SiriusXM. All of this started on a dollar and a dream. We can do anything we want to when we move those mountains out of our head. Nothing worth it comes easy.

If you wait for perfection you will never start.

—April Walker

THE AGILE ENTREPRENEUR

Agility is needed if you want to go the distance.

In life, you need to be able to move fluidly and flow with the changes. Time is moving faster than ever before, and with the globalization of entrepreneurship there are so many things happening in real time that quite honestly, it can be overwhelming. In order to flourish as an entrepreneur, you need to have flexible plans and be able to move forward in uncharted territory, preparing for unforeseen obstacles, and exercising agility.

Adaptation is a necessary ingredient to survive in this digital era. Being able to adapt to change and embrace it is key. Also, the early settlers thrive. Go till the land and plant seeds, because it's easier to grow faster when you're an early adopter, especially when it comes to technology!

#BETHEOCTOPUS.

Build a strong foundation with ancillary branches.
In order to win, you have to be like an octopus these days, having many arms and using them all. You have to grow your branches from your foundation and you need them to work together simultaneously. If you have a BYOB or a business, you have a social media presence and may at the same time be doing some blog guest writing to increase your audience. Maybe you have a podcast and do speaking engagements. If you're selling clothes, you may have an e-commerce store, but you may need to offer tips on social media, and also offer custom to have a point of differentiation. You may need to add an arm that offers a niche service such as styling, or big and tall, and free shipping. You can't just do one thing well anymore, because times have changed. This is a new era, and old behaviors and methods will make you extinct. Some of the things are difficult to measure; however, they are necessary and will foster long-term growth. It may seem tedious now, but they're investments to growing your brand.

#SWINGWITHAIM

SWING WITH AIM.

You can't get a knockout without being able to land your punches. Focus on the target. There's a big world out there. Knowing your niche audience is important, but another key component is understanding exactly what they want. This is a good life skill, period. We all need to become better listeners and target marketers so we can achieve the desired results. Understand what people want and what motivates them.

1. Get crystal-clear on the audience you're serving, being empathetic to their wants and needs, understanding what problems you need to address, and figure out how you create solutions for them.

2. Once you've created solutions, figure out how you will let your audience know. It could be via email newsletters, advertising, social media marketing, webinars, or giving out samples. You want to test-market. You want to generate the solution and make sure you have an audience before you jump the gun and lose too much money. Test marketing first gives you a chance to adjust the plan and retool if necessary before you invest too much on theory alone.

3. Understand where tribe members are. We travel in packs. We like comfort zones, so we tend to hang with like minds. If you're in the music business and marketing to classical music lovers, you don't want to show up at rock concerts! Noooo....find out what events your tribe attends. Is it the food festival, the cannabis industry, or the auto trade show? How much do they spend monthly on average? What are their spending habits?

Once it's clear that you have an audience, conveyed your message, and test-marketed, you can home in on increasing conversions and traffic.

FOUR GEMS TO SWINGING WITH AIM

1. Be clear in your vision—and start with your vision. When you start with your vision and follow your moral compass, you'll be laser focused and everything else will be in alignment. Your internal philosophy will translate into your external world. Your customers will become like extended family because they, too, will believe in your vision and become part of your tribe. Howard Schultz understood this. When he started his Starbucks Coffee empire, he was clear of his vision. With over 22,000 in the world in over 66 countries and growing, he conveyed his message clearly and attracted his tribe members. Inspired by wanting to share the barista experience he observed in Italy, he aimed to bring the romance of the coffee experience to the rest of the world, with a place for conversation and a sense of community. The Starbucks mission is to inspire the human spirit, one person, one cup, and one neighborhood at a time.

2. Make sure you're a symbol of substance. Make sure you are a brand clarifier and that as a BYOB, you (being the symbol) are congruent with your value system. As a company, a symbol should reflect the brand represents from the products to values and philosophy. Example: McDonald's arch, Apple, the Nike swoosh. You know what these symbols represent.

3. SERVE and the people will find you. Remember to make it bigger than you. It's about the people you serve. Whether it's a product or service, it's serving others. Always have an attitude of gratitude and know that you are never bigger than the audience you serve. #servantleadership

4. S.M.A.R.T. GOALS

Developing S.M.A.R.T. (specific, measurable, achievable, relevant, and time bound) goals has turned into a good sound bite, but I ask you to create them with accountability and specificity, whether quarterly and annually, personally or on a professional journey. Assign dates and times to these goals, because then they'll become real and actionable. S.M.A.R.T. goal road maps can guide you with focus and is NOT an abstract outline. The entrepreneurial journey is a long road, and sometimes our plans don't work out the way we want. If we get off track, simply pause and evaluate, notice, and let go. Don't be fast to quit, but instead take a step back with a fresh set of eyes to analyze what changes can be made to the existing plan, before you jump back in and keep going.

You can make necessary adjustments to your goals or eliminate some if necessary, because plans do change. If you really want to take it up a notch, find an accountability partner to hold each other responsible for the assigned goals. Think of your business the same way you think of mastering the Rubik's Cube. Twist, turn, and reconfigure as necessary.

#weisbetterthanme

Teamwork makes the dreamwork and your network creates your net worth.

—Zig Ziglar

#WGTRIBEVIBE

Your team is your tribe. I'll take good hearts with the right attitude over the wrong hearts and attitude with an impressive résumé and accomplished skills any day. Skills can be taught, but you can never teach someone to have a good heart or force a vision that isn't felt. That happens naturally.

It's good to have a diversity of people on your team. You can't gain different perspectives if everyone sees things through the same lens or shares the same experiences. Even though everyone may have a different experience, you want a team that shares one mission. As a leader, being able to listen, process, and exchange information and ideas with your team is essential. Alternatively, if you have a teammate who doesn't believe in the mission and vision, then it's your responsibility to act expeditiously in order to:

1) Keep your vision clear, focused, and moving forward.

2) Not let negative energy spread like the plague internally.

3) Not continue pouring time into a person who isn't a good fit.

Always be diplomatic about other people's ideas, but don't lose sight of your company's vision. When it's YOUR ship, you have the right to dock the ship and let them off.

Always be lavish in your praise. The choice is yours, but I've found that people are motivated when they're celebrated and they spread the love. The more you lift up others, the more you ignite contagious behavior. In the same way, if you're negative, you can also be like Darth Vader, being a real drag and bringing everyone down.

WALKERGEMS

No one likes going into a room of darkness. Stay in the light. Radiate and you will catch a fire. Engage and communicate with them in a positive and loving way. Let them know you care about them and have their back. Find out their interests and ways to connect and make each other better, without scolding or condescending attitudes, but with admiration, love, and respect. Find ways to focus on their strengths, while helping them to manage their weaknesses. They'll receive and may even welcome constructive criticism from this approach. Remember, champions breed champions.

WHAT ABOUT SALES?

Your people determine your product.

—Taso Du Val, cofounder and CEO of Toptal

You are in the service business, period. Whether it's a brand, product, or service, if you're in business, you're the service provider with a leadership role. If you don't want to serve, don't start a business. So many entrepreneurs get this part wrong. We're only conduits, acting as problem solvers for our tribe members. We are here to add to the world and make it better. When you're focused on yourself, it's hard to serve others. You're limiting and setting boundaries for how far your ideas can go and grow. The minute we make it about us and not the people, we limit the possibilities and cut off the blood supply. We stop the circulation. It's impossible to be selfish and significant.

When we live to serve others, we create contagious behavior and our ideas and vision magnify, territories increase, and the people will find us.

HAVE AN ABC SALES PLAN.

Confidence is going after Moby Dick in a rowboat with the tartar sauce.

—Zig Ziglar

You can fine-tune after. It's fantastic to have great, innovative, or groundbreaking products or services, but what does it mean if you can't get them into the marketplace fast enough or become profitable? If you believe in your products and services, you won't ever have to sell because you will just be sharing information and jewels that you want everyone to know about.

You'll want them to share in the experience because it will benefit them as well.

You really need to know HOW you are going to sell, WHO your customer is, and WHERE your products will sell before you start investing in the idea. Once you commit, be aggressive when you think about sales, because this is a business.

When I re-emerged with my Walker Wear brand, I thought my plan was solid. I started with "front-end thinking." The problem was my plan was pretty rigid, without fluidity—I hadn't prepared any other options. I thought that my e-commerce website store would be able to grow the sales gradually, but honestly, my projections weren't realistic. FYI...make sure you're not planning your sales based on how many likes you get on social media, such as Instagram or Facebook.

Likes don't equal sales. You'll need to convert those potential "likers" into sales. How will you get them to your website? Is your website enticing enough for the sale? A staggering 67 percent of my website visitors jumped ship at the shopping cart stage. Can you imagine that? That's painful to think about. These are the kind of holes you have to plug up or figure out fast.

Sales didn't grow as I initially planned, so I had to implement some backend thinking (in a reactionary state) with a plan B and C. If I had prepared an A, B, and C plan in the beginning, perhaps I could've assessed better, implemented more test-marketing, and tried all three plans to see how to execute a balance, resulting in a less costly experience. I could've stabilized and catapulted sales faster. Being fluid and creating multiple choices are necessary in today's climate.

Thankfully, I was able to adjust my plan quickly enough to recover by adding other creative layers such as popups and amplifying my story, while integrating new content and collaborating with other creative brands. This resulted in more visibility and increased sales.

Being a front-end thinker and having back-end thinking skills are both necessary to surviving and thriving. In order to get out of the gate and head towards the goal as fast as possible, we need to have a contingency plan ready, because sometimes we aren't fortunate enough to get a second chance.

#WGBookClub

There are many good sales books out there, but here are two of my favorites:

1. The Secrets of Closing the Sale, by the late and great Zig Ziglar (classic)
2. The Sales Bible, by Jeffrey Gitomer

WALKERGEMS

You miss 100 percent of the shots you don't take.

—Wayne Gretzky

So many people get in their own way. They're trapped in their own heads. They put so much pressure on themselves, romanticizing what it should be like, and end up talking themselves out of their dream before they start or procrastinating because they think they have to wait until everything is perfect. They think they need a 40 page business plan or a big deluxe office or a big team…they think they need to have it all figured it out before they start. These are self-inflicted excuses.

If you have a vision, create a road map, and begin. You know it's real. You can describe the potential audience, where they shop, how they spend, and can explain their value system. You've done the homework. Look at your vision with fluidity. When you turn on the faucet, the water starts flowing…the ideas just start flowing and shaping. The beginning is the formation process. You'll start seeing progress toward the middle…although not necessarily in the beginning. You never know everything, especially not in the beginning. That's the magic of self-discovery. Trust the process. It's essential.

You're either participating or sitting on the sidelines.

Do you ever notice that the ones that get involved in anything early become the experts and considered the authorities first? They usually catch the wave coming instead chasing it.

Go and grow through it. You'll constantly discover, learn, encounter obstacles, and become the master, turning your experience into a successful business. Exercising this behavior allows you to execute, transform, and monetize businesses much faster than those who stay paralyzed. In other words, the early adopters who arrive at the party first position themselves with the best seats.

Early settlers know what it takes, building a base, and figuring the strategy. Anything worth doing takes time and has risks associated, so doing your due diligence and homework is an essential ingredient when ascertaining potential new ventures. When you weigh out the risks, also consider the cost of inaction. Not taking action can be even costlier.

We have a chance to plant seeds and make our pastures greener and more fruitful. Whatever you do, research, assess, make decisions, and give 100 percent.

#goallout or #gohome

WALKERGEMS

#WGTRUESTORY

I remember many years ago I was working with Mike Tyson in Las Vegas and one of the Team Tyson members invited my team to attend a presentation and meeting for a potential business opportunity. We were told Les Brown would be there and was going to present. We came to the meeting excited, and before the meeting started, a woman brought out a life-size picture of Les Brown to the middle of the floor, and then his voice started—as a tape recording. We thought this was hysterical. Obviously, this was a loooong time ago...lol. We didn't take the meeting seriously after that and couldn't focus on the opportunity being presented in front of us because we were so distracted by this presentation. We automatically dismissed it. The opportunity turned out to be for one of the first satellite television providers just starting. It wasn't even on the map yet, and we had a chance to be involved with this business. Can you imagine? We didn't do our homework and completely missed the opportunity to be early settlers in a very lucrative situation.

Don't make the same mistake I did. You need to know how to separate the wheat from the chaff and learn to discern what is valuable and useful from what is worthless. (Matthew 3:12). Seize the right opportunities with a vengeance.

Whenever you find yourself on the side of the majority, it's time to pause and reflect.

—Mark Twain

BUILD YOUR ADVERSITY MUSCLES TO GO THE DISTANCE.

In your life, it's necessary to be a three in one…your own coach, cheerleader, and always a student. As an entrepreneur, tough skin is a prerequisite. You have to be able to withstand more failure than success, more upsets than wins, and more rejection than acceptance. Can you handle that? Take note that not everyone will agree with you or understand the road you're traveling, and some will think that you need to change your vision, give up, or simply won't believe in you. That's OK. When you win, the naysayers will become the yaysayers.

True story. I can remember everyone telling me what I couldn't accomplish. There were lots of opinionated people advising me that I wouldn't be able to compete with major, more established brands at that time. I was told my price points shouldn't be as high as my competition and that as a female designer in a menswear business, I couldn't make it. I chose to be selectively ignorant and processed the information that I needed to discover or retain while ignoring the negativity or opinions without merit. I listened to my inner voice. Rely on what you know to be your truth and focus on the reason you started. Trust your own magic.

Be prepared to pick yourself up when you fall and brush your knees off, but keep going. Know how to dust that dirt off your shoulders and smile, even when people don't believe in you. Never take it personally because it's not their journey to walk, it's yours. In the same way, it's not their job to believe, it's yours. "Everything ain't for everybody." You just keep on having faith, building adversity muscles, and the rest will fall in place.

"Always be true to yourself but mindful to others."
@shelikes2014

NETWORK

Life is about networking. We are independent, yet interdependent. From the time we're born, we are connected to each other. We need each other. As we travel through life and set out on our entrepreneurial path, the same connection applies. We constantly meet other people who help us connect the dots.

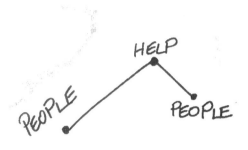

One of the most important things in this life is to honor and respect people, no matter who they are, irrespective of job titles or positions, race, creed, or religion. We should all be treated with good cheer and dignity. It's a life practice that will not only keep you in good spirits but spreading good energy, making the world a better place. Treating everyone with respect not only builds character but it also creates consistency, trustworthiness, and a reliable reputation. Trustworthy people are memorable. Now add your skills to the equation, and you will open more doors. Truth be told, sometimes you may not even have the skills, but a blessing will just drop out of the sky because someone referred you because of your character.

An excellent read on building relationships and communicating with others is a classic book that will never go out of style called "How to Win Friends and Influence People," by Dale Carnegie. This timeless classic is a basic that is packed with so many life gems, including essential principles that will help us communicate more effectively, and offers good information for our journey. For some, it may serve as a reminder of things that we used to know but that we may have forgotten. Either way, whether you're just starting out or it's serving as a refresher, it's a worthy read with good takeaways.

WALKERGEMS

#relationshipgoals

Every opportunity in life that you encounter comes through a relationship. It's either one that already exists or it may be a new encounter. We live in a great time when you can collaborate on your ideas or "Voltron" them into something even greater with the right partnerships. The relationships you establish can unfold and create new projects and opportunities and open new doors that you can't even imagine. They can take you to amazing new levels. Be willing to collaborate with other companies that want to achieve the same mission or reach the same goals. Find common intersections. The most successful people are independent and interdependent.

Things to consider when building relationships:

Honorable Intentions

Relationships first! #InsideOut

Community.

(We are all connected.)

Strategic partnerships. (Build those relationships.)

Globalization of Entrepreneurship.

(The world is smaller than ever and you can connect and collaborate with worldwide players.)

be a
transformer

WALKER♥GEMS

The fastest way to change yourself is to hang out with people who are already the way you want to be.

—Reid Hoffman,
cofounder of LinkedIn

The beauty of life is that we get to choose our relationships and how we engage with people. We can discern where and how we spend our time and who we spend it with. Since time is our most precious asset, we want to invest wisely. From internships to coaches and mentors, colleagues, peers, and your audience, people can help you either light a fire or put it out. The way you treat people will make the difference in whether they'll cushion your fall or get out the way. Create valuable relationships. Make it a point to seek out relationships and connect with folks who will stretch you, hold you accountable, and support you. Never ask for what you can't give: Be willing to reciprocate the same behavior. I knew that my handshake was the most important thing in my life. Word is bond. People trust what you do and not what you say. Your actions will dictate your reputation. Your reputation will be a strong factor in determining your opportunities. Opportunities don't always knock on your door. Sometimes you have to go knocking on many doors and even be willing to kick them in.

I can't overstate the importance of building relationships. They can open so many doors and new chapters for you. Networking and building relationships requires you to leave your comfort zone and leave the nest. Are you willing to introduce yourself and walk up to strangers? I remember I'd show up at every event and concert, and knock on those entertainment company doors. I'd approach them, introduce myself, hand out cards, and invite them to check out my fashion. I'd find out where my #wgtribevibe was and find a way to get there. I'd get my hustle on. I wasn't afraid to create a circle of influencers with creative, innovative, and gifted people that shared that same kind of energy. I'd strike up conversations to find out where our interests converged. People could feel my sincerity as an enthusiast and lover of hip-hop, fashion, and entrepreneurship. When you're genuinely interested in people, you'll discover each other's interests, passions, and common ground. Over time, you'll build trust. Be patient. Worthwhile relationships take time, because we need to check out a person's integrity, character, and motives and tend to gravitate to like tribe members.

Over time, as I developed these business relationships, people inquired about my fashion styles and services, and once given the opportunity, I made sure to overdeliver. I put my foot in each design, crafting style and quality with the "wow factor." Being a straight shooter with a standup character will forge the genuine and valued relationships. My relationships have introduced me to priceless opportunities, including traveling this world and sitting under the stars in Cuba with some of the most interesting and legendary people of our times. In my lifetime, I've been blessed to develop some amazing relationships, and through them, I've worked with some of the greatest artists in history such as Biggie, Tupac, Aaliyah, Jay Z, and style icons like RUN-DMC and Naughty by Nature.

I love that I've been able to remain true to myself. Remember, people are smart. We can smell a phony from a mile away. As my girl Davida Arnold, the founder and CEO #GirlGameChanger, says, "Always be yourself, otherwise you're a stranger to yourself, and that's just weird."

Who you partner up with or collaborate with may be more important than who you hire.

#LovenoteforU

If you have a dream, if you want to magnify it and make it bigger than yourself, you're going to need to create a tribe and build some relationships. Nothing significant happens without relationships. Reach out to people who can help you stand taller, identify networking events, conferences, mentorships, and be willing to mingle with other pros. It's OK to feel a little awkward in a new situation. Be comfortable with being uncomfortable. This is how we go and grow to new heights and create unimaginable "pinch yourself" experiences.

YOU ARE YOUR OWN COMPETITION.

We are really competing against ourselves, we have no control over how other people perform.

—Pete Cashmore,
founder and CEO of Mashable

We've all heard "comparison is the thief of joy." Instead of comparing, look in the mirror and compete with that person. Don't look to the left or the right. Work on your own masterpiece. Be the best version of yourself and strive to be better than you were yesterday. That should be your measuring stick. Don't worry about others. There will always be someone ahead of you in life, and there's always someone waiting to get your spot, but who cares? When you focus on those people, a few things can happen. You can't give 100 percent because you're not focusing on the road in front of you but instead on peripheral views. Think about running in a relay race. You're specifically told not to look back or from side to side. You're told to look straight ahead, so you don't slow down and can focus on the road ahead of you. All you're supposed to do is put your hand out while you running to pass the baton, but you DO NOT LOOK BACK. The same is true in life. When you don't look straight ahead, other thoughts can seep into your mind because your attention is being divided and there are distractions. You lose steam.

SOMETIMES IT'S THE THING YOU WANT TO DO THE LEAST, YOU NEED TO DO THE MOST.

Do that and you're already halfway there.

TAKE IN EVERY SINGLE MOMENT OF THE JOURNEY.

Every stage of the process is special. The beginning and the end are exciting, but truthfully, it's the muddy middle stage, the gritty grind and the hustle, where you'll spend the most time in life and in your business. Ironically, it's often at this stage that we take the most for granted, because we're too consumed with anticipation of our future, and as a result, we're not fully living in the present. "Right now" in this moment is part of your journey. The present has a lesson. Every time I've had the luck of tackling big mountains, it was great to reach the top, and I've always been appreciative, but it was the time that was spent getting up those mountains, encountering obstacles, and gaining the invaluable lessons for the wins that were priceless.

Teamwork skills, developing tough skin, and tenacity are discovered in this stage. This is how we become. That "mind over matter" mantra takes on a whole new meaning when you go through the muddy middle stage. This process is amazing for any entrepreneur, but it's also true of life in general.

Stay in the present, because you want to soak up life's lessons. They comprise the ingredients to your story. Don't miss the moments with your focus being somewhere else. Always keep gratitude in your heart while you're trying to get to your destination, and it will make you feel much more alive and appreciative on your journey. You'll become better... not bitter. Your wins will be even sweeter.

Slow down, and everything you are chasing will come around and catch you.

—John De Paola

#NoDoOvers

P.S. Remember, there are no do-overs. This day will never arrive again, so make sure to stay in the present and make the most of each day. The journey really is the destination. One never knows the hour.

THIS DIGITAL ERA

The real problem is not whether machines think but whether men do.

—B.F. Skinner

You have to be part of the paradigm shift and keep your mind keen. Don't overthink or become so intimidated that you don't jump into the changes taking place in our society. When you make assumptions without information or facts, you create self-imposed barriers and usually will make a molehill into a mountain in your mind, and find excuses. This also can be a defense mechanism and a scarcity mindset. You're working from a small and limited thought process. You also run the risk of becoming old news fast, or passé, using excuses like "I'm not going to get on social media because it's stupid or "I don't want people to know my business" or "I don't see why I have to get on social media." If you've said this before, or have a friend who has these opinions, then these extinction club thoughts will classify you as a member of "the lost ones." #adinosaur. The ways people communicate, market, research, engage, and sell are now online. It's where you find global opportunities and network in real time. We're not going backwards. We've hit this third sector of technology, and the world is never going to reverse. In fact, time is moving exponentially with the advancements of technology and automated systems, apps, and loads of other gadgets. The longer you wait to jump in, the more difficult it is to catch up.

BEING SOCIAL

Run your biz by thinking about the future, not living in the past.

Social media is a strange beast. It's somewhat of an illusion. It's a social outlet, very lucrative, and you can use it as a tool to leverage for your business. The #InstaFamous celebrities who have created large followings on social media or become influencers are selling their own products, and some are profiting from affiliate sales/marketing and making bundles with product placements or amassing and building their email lists. It's big business. They've learned the power of BYOB (Be Your Own Brand). If you're spending a lot of time on social media, make it work for you; otherwise, analyze the time you're spending there. While a lot of us are studying pretty pictures, real life is happening. A lot of these pretty pictures on social media have become like the reality shows…scripted for entertainment purposes. Don't spend too much time making deposits where there is no return. You have to invest in yourself and manage the time you're investing elsewhere.

Side note: Social media can be a useful tool or a distraction to your life. Take inventory of how much time you spend on social media and why. For our own sanity, we need to choose information we retain and what to ignore. After you take your own assessment, you may decide to downsize the amount of social media time and invest more time in your continued self-development.

Social media tip: At least grab your name online, if you have a business. The domain name is very inexpensive and you can get social names and sit on them. It's always better to be safe than sorry. True story: I had a radio personality friend who would always use a certain term, and it was gaining some serious traction. He decided to do an online show, and when he went to secure the name, it wasn't available because someone took the domain name and was holding it. They beat him to it, but worse, they asked $50,000 for the name because they knew he'd already marketed it and made it famous. They thought he wanted it that bad. He did want it badly, but not for $50,000. Lesson learned.

**ALLOT YOURSELF A PASS FOR A CERTAIN AMOUNT OF TIME ON SOCIAL MEDIA AND STICK TO IT.

BE A DISRUPTER

You have to be in it to win it.

So many people are living in the past. If you're operating your business and making decisions based on today, you're already late. Remember when Apple went to Sony with iTunes and shared its vision, but because of conflict, internal factors, and a lack of vision, Sony didn't move fast enough for the technology revolution that was coming? What happened? The movement ended up happening anyway, but Sony missed the opportunity to participate in a much bigger way by not being proactive early on. They tried to play catch up by launching their own iTunes like service called Sony Connect in May of 2004 and shut down just three years later. Time is moving too fast. We need to be predicting, forecasting, and staying ahead of the curve. Tap into your imagination. This is how we have to run our businesses now more than ever before. There's a tremendous opportunity for us to engage, connect, and amplify our messaging to our audience. We can observe and assess to understand what our tribe members want. We can crowdsource and receive valuable information and feedback from our audiences in real time on social media, but we have to get in the game.

At every moment, that's the opportunity. Have you ever noticed that the players that practice and hone their skills and engage in new techniques and level up will excel while others that don't stretch their skills or change up can stay stuck, stagnant, and on the sidelines? Take LeBron James, for example. We know he is a phenomenon, but when he spoke about the Cavaliers championship, he said some things I found very interesting. LeBron explained that they were playing in a way that wasn't working for him or the team in the first half of the finals. He had to re-evaluate, and then he analyzed the tapes and attacked the game in a different way, implementing new techniques that propelled the Cavaliers to not only a comeback but to the championship. We can all take heed of this forward-moving philosophy in life, especially regarding the new tools that exist.

WHAT'S IN YOUR TOOLBOX?

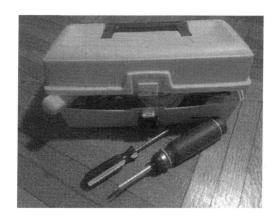

#learnersareearners

Learning how to use the tools of today will help you navigate, steer, and amplify your brand or career. If used effectively, these tools can help automate your life as well. Below is a toolbox kit of some helpful resources for you. While these are suggestions, I encourage you to do your own research and homework to explore other options that make you more efficient and stretch your horizons or keep you sprouting.

***Below has some of my tools and discoveries.

APPS

Expensify ($)

Venmo ($)

Square ($)

PayPal ($)

Shopify (e-commerce mobile/web shopping platform)

Dropbox (content space saver)

WeTransfer (shares large files)

iMovie (visual tool, films and photos)

Periscope (social media, live content)

Facebook Live (social media, live content)

Youtube (social media, shows)

Google Hangout (group video conferencing)

Zoom (group video conferencing)

Instagram (social media, sales)

Facebook (social media, sales)

Buffer (manage all your social media, scheduling)

Hootsuite (manage all your social media, scheduling)

Photoshop (design editing tool)

Fiverr (creative outsourcing)

Canva (creative templates for everything)

Pixabay (free amazing stock photos)

Informative/Inspirational Podcasts

Trafficandsales.com

lewishowes.com

michaelhyatt.com

www.chalenejohnson.com

The #AskGaryVee Show

fourhourworkweek.com

Shopify podcasts

etthehiphoppreacher

**It's important for me to note that at this time, I am not affiliated with any of the following organizations but have tested all of the products or listened to the podcasts. I believe #sharingicscaring and these all have been helpful on my journey.

#TRANSPARENCY

"Transparency" is the new "in" word. We don't need to "tell all" on social media. Some things are better left mysterious. We should be selective when sharing our content. Your content should be relevant to your brand and page, and if you've decided to #BYOB, you should offer value that is congruent to your messaging. You should decide your transparency settings for the content that you wish to execute. You can be honest but general or you don't have to tell the story. Discern what's appropriate. Ask yourself if the content is a good fit for the personality of your brand. Decide what kind of vibes you want to share with the world.

We don't want to be sold or told anymore. We want you to share. You have to be authentic in your experience. We want to know that "you say what you mean and you mean what you say." You should admit when you make a mistake, be responsible, and remain humble. Being flawsome can be awesome because people want "relatable." People who are transparent about their wins, failures, and flaws connect on a deeper level. Think about the people you resonate with and why. No one wants perfection. It's not trustworthy.

Foster inclusiveness, but understand that once you've mapped out your social media content plan and you share the information, that content is transparent to the universe forever. We are being audited more than ever, from potential and strategic corporate or affiliate partners to employers to your schools. Social media has changed the game. Consider yourself warned.

All labor that uplifts humanity has dignity and importance and should be undertaken with painstaking excellence.

—Martin Luther King

ADD VALUE.

Today we are inundated with so much information, countless promises. We hear everything under the sun. There is an online gold rush occurring. We are told to download this and sign up for that webinar to learn to make $1 million in the next 30 days…lol. In these times with so much information and access at our fingertips, strangely enough, a lot of us are rejecting the actual information. I recently read an article by Andy Borowitz in the New Yorker magazine that stated "scientists have discovered a powerful new strain of fact-resistant humans who are threatening the ability of earth to sustain life, a sobering new study reports." Even this book! I constructed it this way because I wanted to be social media friendly, since this is where these daily #walkergems were born, but I really felt the need to make it convenient and travel size on purpose, so it can be a quick read and easy to stash. Folks want to get what they need and they want it now. It doesn't need to be overwhelming or packaged with a bow. They just need you to address their pain points. Share your experience, give 100 percent, and provide value as much as you can, because we always want to feel like we got a bonus and we appreciate it. We recognize the people who care, and it's a good way for you to stand out and build long-lasting loyalty. We all want to feel like we just found the Cracker Jack prize inside of the box or got a little more than we anticipated.

Don't be worried about the numbers on social media. Just stay focused on your niche, seeking to offer substance to your tribe. Shoot for excellence, provide insight with value, share your experience, and you'll attract the right #wgtribevibe. Your audience will grow over time and you will have loyalists. I'd rather have a really engaged and connected #wgtribevibe audience with like minds than a big audience of people that don't care.

If you have a brand or biz, here's a good tip for posting. Before you post, take a hard look at your post. If it's not something you would stop to look at if you were someone else and want to read or repost, then don't post it. Be considerate of how many times you post a day. I try to never post more than one to three times a day for my brands.

Have the courage to follow your heart and intuition. They somehow know what you truly want to become.

—Steve Jobs

#DOITFORTHECULTURE

A culture creator is someone who is an ideator and adds to the world. They create belief systems and take chances that transform into culture. These ideas are adopted and owned by everyone. Culture is an inward-outward process. I've noticed that it starts with something organic that comes to fruition over time. People gravitate toward it because they're like-minded. You'll find that the way you execute your appearance, convey your principles and belief system, communicate, or create all will send a message to the world. Your internal practices will manifest to your external world, so make sure the two are interdependent and congruent. You want to develop a company that reflects your philosophy, values, and standards to the world. It should be an extension of you.

We're all a part of a herd or a pack, but some will be the visionaries and some will be the teammates and tribe members. Both are essential. We all have different roles and assignments, and honestly, life would be boring if everyone was the same. There is something magical and magnetic that happens when everyone can pull together, sharing the same vision, purpose, with enthusiasm and passion.

Shared views, values, goals, and social practices shape a company's culture over time. Know the DNA of your company and make sure that everyone has the same "blood type" as yours. These internal principles can create contagious behavior externally. As your company arm extends, you will find that your customers reaching out to connect will be of that same tribe. The vision and mission should always be bigger than one person. Always make your reason or cause bigger than you, learn to serve, and the people will find you.

GRAB YOUR BULLHORN

Be your own press publicist. In today's world, it's getting tougher and tougher for a publicist. They're competing with blogs and digital platforms that can also send out news in real time at a moment's notice. This represents a tremendous opportunity for us, in developing #BYOB. If you're a solopreneur or a symphony, you have a chance to beat your own chest. You can grab your own bullhorn.

You can start via social media and learn the how to's, such as writing media alerts and press releases for pitching. Social media gives you the chance to start engaging directly and start building relationships via Twitter, Facebook, Instagram, and so on. Connect with people. Find common interests—people are usually inquisitive. Build relationships. Learn how to be a storyteller because you're unique and your content is your asset. Take the time to learn how to package your why and share your journey and your process. Be inclusive.

Have you ever heard that content is king? It's because we can't get enough of it. Everyone is rooting for the underdog, and there has never been a better time to be an entrepreneur.

Until you have a team, you need to be super creative. Create a fictitious character if you have to. Set up another email address for your "publicist" and then use that email for all of your pitches. Get in where you fit in and figure it out. Sometimes it takes being like the Wizard of Oz, being the man behind the curtain, until you can get your weight up.

You've always had the power my dear, you just had to learn it for yourself.

–Glenda, Wizard of Oz

Stepping

Up

Consistently

Chiseling

Excellence

Sowing

Seeds

DON'T MAKE YOURSELF SMALL TO MAKE SOMEONE ELSE FEEL BIG.

Don't ever dim your light to make others comfortable or just to fit in. You weren't born to fit in. You have an assignment. It starts and ends with you. If any situation makes you feel uncomfortable, less than, or unworthy, it needs to be changed. Realize that when someone else uncomfortable with you, it's probably not about you but more about their own issues. Don't feed into that negative energy and give it life and don't even think about becoming a chameleon in order to fit someone else's box. Just be yourself, the best version of you, and hold your head high. Push those shoulders back and strut your stuff. Stand tall. Act like it's already yours. Your words and actions need to give power to the dream until it's your reality. Be the best possible version of yourself. That's what you are here to do.

A person who walks in another's tracks leaves no footprint.

—Proverb

SOMETHING TO REMEMBER - SUCCESS IS ELUSIVE.

It's like chasing a butterfly. My advice is to focus on the journey and stay in the present because that's all we can control. In the now, we get to ideate the lives we imagined; we chase and are actually realizing those dreams. We get to sculpt and craft them daily. That is the real Lotto ticket. If we're waiting to get to the destination before we feel like we've achieved success or can be happy, then we will be sadly disappointed.

In my best moments and memories, it was all of the hustle and bustle with muscle and those team efforts that I remember most. I can remember those days when I was running through airports trying to make the plane with a big trunk of samples vividly or when I was at my first trade show in Las Vegas. We didn't have money for a booth at the trade show, so I rented a suite at a hotel that had dark lighting with old and very "Vegas" furniture that would remind you of a cheap version of a suite in the movie Casino…gaudy and tacky, think plastic on blue velveteen couches. My team and I made the best of it and got creative.

We rolled up our sleeves, stayed up all night, and converted our suite into a Walker Wear popup showroom. That night we worked so late that when we took a break, there was nowhere else for our crew to hit but the drive-thru at McDonald's, or actually, maybe that was our budget, because we were in Vegas. The next day buyers started visiting our suite, and then the next day we didn't know what to expect but we sold and sold and sold. We had the best time of our lives. In the end, what I can remember most is the laughter and snapping on each other all night while we worked, and the drive-thru lady who insisted on giving us extra fries at Mickey D's. Those are the moments that you will remember that matter. Everything else is gravy.

I AM, I CAN, I WILL

We all hold riches inside of us. It's difficult for me to watch an individual with so much potential stay paralyzed by their fears or not tap into their gifts. Being an entrepreneur is like being a superhero. It takes a special breed, but everyone can BYOB and act accordingly. You get what you command. Be collaborative, spread your wings, level up, and hone your skills. Don't be intimidated to be different and swim with the sharks because that's what it's going to take to get there. You can do this. #iCan #iWill #iAmEnough #itsDone #growth

But someone will say, "You have faith and I have works." Show me your faith apart from your works, and I will show you my faith by my works. -James 2:18

WALKERGEMS

Thank you for allowing me to share my God given gifts, experience, wins and failures with the world. To my parents, thanks for always believing in us and teaching us how to dream big. To my family who supports and loves me endlessly, my cup runneth over. I'm so thankful for the friends who are in my life that motivate me and continue to propel me forward. Peg Northrop, what would I have done without your literary advice and wisdom? Appreciate you. Peggy Nauts, thank you. Afahari Mku OrisaYomi Efundeji, thank you so much for your advice and help sis. Myorr Janha, Russell Simmons, Misa Hylton, Datwon Thomas, and Rosie Perez, I appreciate your kind words and support so much. To the angels who continue to support me along the way, thank you. To my #tribevibe, you inspire me to keep giving. Giving feels so good. YOU'RE THE BEST.

#WGTRIBE

RESOURCES

#BYOB (Be your own brand)

(What do you want to be? p. 14) - In preparing these notes, I actually crowdsourced from my personal Facebook Survey in December of 2016.

(Facts from the Anatomy of an Entrepreneur (p.16-17): I'm indebted to research from a report produced in 2009 by the Kauffman Report.`

(The facts on the startup survival rate, p.38): According to the Small Business Administration, about two-thirds of businesses with employees survive at least two years and about half survive at least five years were found via the SBA Small Business Facts or at

https://www.sba.gov/sites/default/files/Business-Survival.pdf.

Find your tribe members: https://www.meetup.com

EDX – founded by Harvard and MIT in 2012—a great online learning destination.

In preparing the "Five Great Failure Stories," I utilized the following resources:

Walt Disney (The Animated Man: A Life of Walt Disney, by Michael Barrier, p. 35-38)

(Decide & Conquer: The Ultimate Guide for Improving Your Decision Making, by Stephen Robins, p 157)

Oprah Winfrey (performing Under pressure: The Science of Doing Your Best When It Matters Most, by Hendrie Weisenger, J.p Pauliw-Fry)

George Steinbrenner and the Yankees (George Steinbrenner and the Yankees, The T Files, New York Times, He's Back and He's Still the Boss, by Douglas Martin, October 25, 1992)

Milton Hershey (Biography.com, Milton Hershey, 1857-1945)

Colonel Sanders (In praise of failure: The Value of Overcoming Mistakes in Sports and in Life, by Mark H. Anshel, xvii)

The Sony/ iTunes story (is based from the study novels information on page 173-174)

http://www.studynovels.com/Book/Pages?bookId=578&pageNo=124

The LeBron story told about changing up his game was from an interview after he won the championship against the Golden Warriors.

"Scientists have discovered a powerful new strain of fact-resistant humans who are threatening the ability of earth to sustain life, a sobering new study reports" is from a New Yorker magazine article written by Andy Borowitz.

The statement "Who you partner up with may be more important than who you hire" was a sentiment that Steve Case spelled out as a speaker discussing the different sectors of technology of the first, second, and this third wave of technology at a South by Southwest convention. I strongly agree with this statement.

Starbucks Information and statistical information was found at

https://www.starbucks.com/about-us/company-information

https://news.starbucks.com/news/coffee-traditions-around-the-world

My reference of "67 percent abandoned cart sales" was analytics and research done from my website. (Shopify)

My satellite reference story actually occurred in Las Vegas in 1996.

The information that people on average check Facebook from their mobile devices 14 times daily is from a NBC News study, nbcnews.com, March 28, 2013, by Nidhi Subbaraman.

The Quote ("The days are long but the years are short"p.54) Reference from The Gretchin project Michael Jordan on missing shots (Chicago Tribune, "Without Failure, Jordan Would Be False Idol", by Eric Zorn - May 19,1997)

The statistics that "only twelve percent of the founders of Inc. 500 companies conducted formal market research before their launch and forty percent wrote business plans, and of those that wrote plans, two-thirds of them admitted they got rid of them later." – (was a reference from "Seat of the pants" according to Sarah Bartlett, Oct. 15, 2002)

I'm indebted to Guy Routte of War Media for sharing his story.

I'm grateful to Reggie Ossé for graciously sharing his story.

YOU TUBE

My Morning Visualization Exercise

https://www.youtube.com/watch?v=856BTxtPW80

BIBLE

"Consider it pure joy, my brothers and sisters, whenever you face trials of many kinds, because you know that the testing of your faith produces perseverance." (James 1:2-4)

"Now faith is substance of things hoped for, the evidence of things not seen." (Hebrews 11:1)

"You need to know how to separate the wheat from the chaff and learn to discern what is valuable and useful from what is worthless." (referencing from a scripture in Matthew 3:12)

But someone will say, "You have faith and I have works." Show me your faith apart from your works, and I will show you my faith by my works. -James 2:18

OTHER NOTES

Jay Z – My observation of Jay's determination came firsthand as I watched him on his climb. Jay-Z put in the work and stayed determined for several years before he became the "success story" to the rest of the world.

BOOK REFERENCES

The Happiness Project, by Gretchen Rubin

The Compound Effect, by Darren Hardy

Start With Why, by Simon Sinek

The 7 Habits of Highly Effective People, by Stephen Covey

The Other "F" Word, by John Danner and Mark Coopersmith

The Sales Bible, by Jeffrey Gitomer

How to Win Friends and Influence People, by Dale Carnegie

ABOUT THE AUTHOR

@iamaprilwalker @walkerwear @walkergems

http://iamaprilwalker.com/pages/walkergems

Brooklyn Baby!

April Walker is a Brooklyn native. This savvy entrepreneur and motivator is one of the givers and game changers who inspired an urban fashion lifestyle category that became a multi-billion dollar industry with her fashion brand "Walker Wear." As a brand evangelist, her company, "A.Walker Group" has worked with many clients domestically and internationally throughout the years. Daily you can find Walker spreading her "Walkergems" via social media. The purpose of these Walkergems is to empower, inspire and ignite the spirit of entrepreneurship by giving people the tools they need to design the lives they imagine and uplift our communities in the process. "By nurturing innovative talent, today's entrepreneurs and visionaries are one step closer to realizing their dreams."

For inquiries on speaking engagements, trade shows, and events, email **contact@walkergems.com**

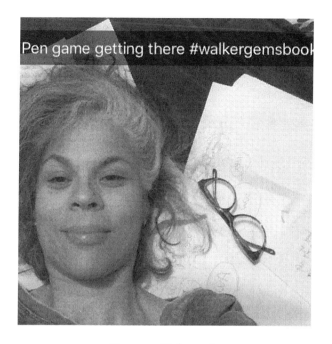

Pen game getting there #walkergemsbook

Next up. Volume 2.

"Now Let's Get Down To Business"

WALKERGEMS

420 Clinton Avenue, Brooklyn, NY 11238
Copyright and Published 2017

ISBN: 1542484782
ISBN-13: 9781542484787

For information on special discounts on bulk purchases, for speaking engagements, or to book an event, please email contact@walkergems.com.

Designed by April Walker

Manufactured in the United States of America

PICTURE CREDITS

Unless otherwise stated all images are courtesy April Walker. Any inadvertent omissions can be rectified in the future. Original artwork is by Jack Walker or April Walker. Cover artwork concept by Jack Walker.

Made in the USA
Monee, IL
23 February 2020